Extraordinary YOU

A Woman's Guide to Having it All

Extraordinary YOU

A Woman's Guide to Having it All

Megan Wolfenden

Disclaimer

All the information, techniques, skills and concepts contained within this publication are of the nature of general comment only and are not in any way recommended as individual advice. The intent is to offer a variety of information to provide a wider range of choices now and in the future, recognising that we all have widely diverse circumstances and viewpoints. Should any reader choose to make use of the information contained herein, this is their decision, and the contributors (and their companies), authors and publishers do not assume any responsibilities whatsoever under any condition or circumstances. It is recommended that the reader obtain their own independent advice.

First Edition 2013

Copyright © 2013 by Megan Wolfenden

All rights reserved. No part of this publication may be reproduced, stored in a retrieval system, or transmitted in any form or by any means, electronic, mechanical, photocopying, recording or otherwise, without the prior written permission from the publisher.

National Library of Australia Cataloguing-in-Publication entry:

Wolfenden, Megan, author.

Extraordinary YOU: A Woman's Guide to Having it All / Megan Wolfenden

ISBN: 9780987494702 (paperback)

Self-actualization (Psychology)
Success.
Finance, Personal.
Business.

158.1

Testimonials

"According to demographers, the only way to solve global poverty (and increase our chances for creating world peace) is to empower girls and women through education. Imagine if we could offer women education that comes free and is coupled with economic opportunity? This is the mission Megan Wolfenden has been on for many years through her network marketing business.

My wish is for her book to spread quickly and widely because women everywhere are waiting for her message of hope and possibility."

Dr. Josephine Gross
Editor in Chief, Networking Times
Dean of Faculty, Networking University

"Every woman has the ability to achieve what she wants; to live the life of her dreams. This book will help you to unlock your potential and become everything you deserve to be. A positive, fun and truly inspiring book."

June Dally-Watkins OAM
Founder, CEO education and Training
Business finishing college
Ambassador-at-large, Crossroads Foundation

Special Offers

For updated booklists, seminar locations and current special offers go to:

This book is available at special quantity discounts for bulk purchases to be included for **marketing, promotions, fundraisers and or educational purposes**.

Free chapters are also available to promote to your clients or give away as a gift with the option to purchase the full Print or Digital copy of the book.

Contact **megan@extraordinaryyou.net** to discuss how we can accommodate your needs. Or visit our website at http://extraordinaryyou.net

About Megan Wolfenden

Megan is an award-winning businesswoman who travels the world teaching people how to build their own business and reach their full potential. She is passionate about education and inspiring people to retire from their jobs to create successful businesses for themselves and their families. It was this passion that led her to write her first book.

Megan started her career in banking, finance and the computer industry before relocating from Sydney, Australia, to the United States for her husband's work and a new adventure for Megan. While in the US she began building a real estate portfolio, investing in gas, oil, gold, venture capital and other assets, and learning about network marketing.

After 10 years abroad Megan and her husband returned to Australia with their two young sons, both born in California. In 2005 Megan retired from the workforce because she was making more money from her part-time network marketing business than her job. Her multi-million dollar business now operates out of 17 countries.

Megan lives on a beautiful two-acre, waterfront property on the Gold Coast with her husband Anthony, their sons Peter and Sam and their puppy Molly.

Dedication

I dedicate this book to my three wonderful boys – Anthony, Pete and Sam. They inspire me every day. I love you with all my heart.

Megan Wolfenden

Acknowledgements

At a seminar a few years ago the speaker said, 'Everyone has a book inside them waiting to come out'. I didn't believe it at the time but that line stayed in my mind and at a recent wealth creation seminar this book began to surface. With no experience in book writing, I immediately called my friend Fiona Jones and asked, 'How do I write this book?' Fiona helped me get started and recommended experts in editing, publishing and distribution and 'voila', this book became a reality. Thank you Fiona!

Rebecca Griffin, you really helped me breathe life into the script. You have been such an inspiration and delight to work with. You live an extraordinary life and I look forward to watching your new adventures. Sophie Malone and Ruth Benjamin-Thomas, I am so glad at least some people have exceptional skills with English, but more importantly – thanks for your friendship.

My loving husband, Anthony, is always encouraging me to do what I love. With his support, encouragement and great ideas, this book has come to life. He is great at bringing out the best in me and for that I will be eternally grateful. Our two young boys inspire me to be and do more. I thank them for their patience and understanding but most of all their love. I am in awe of everything they do and get the greatest pleasure out of watching them learn and grow. They are my inspiration.

To my wonderful family and friends - thank you. I feel so blessed to be part of your lives. Together we make life FUN. I know all of you are leaving your legacies and making the world a better place. I Love You!

Contents

Introduction		1
How to use this book		3
Chapter 1	Wealth – what does it mean to you?	5
Chapter 2	It's time to dream	39
Chapter 3	Creating sources of income	73
Chapter 4	Happy families – fulfiling relationships	103
Chapter 5	Spiritual abundance	123
Chapter 6	Women's health	143
Chapter 7	Never stop learning	157
Chapter 8	The act of giving	177
Chapter 9	Bring it all together and make it happen	189
Appendix 1	Book club	210
Appendix 2	Recommended reading list	213

Introduction

Throughout my lifetime I have spent quality time with so many incredible women. These ladies have freely shared their life's trials and successes with me and we have offered each other support and ideas in an effort to help each other through the tough times. Again and again I see women breaking through barriers to achieve incredible things. They all seem to be striving for love, peace and a little bit of fun in their lives. Success is different for each of us but we all recognise when someone is meeting their goals and enjoying themselves and the lives they have created. I wanted to write this book as a gift to all women. A quick insight into what might be possible and some ideas on how to get started creating the life they dream of.

As I write this section I am sitting in a 6000 square foot (557 square metres) home in Squaw Valley, California, for our annual family ski holiday. As luck would have it, this house is twice the size and prestige as the one we paid for due to two upgrades. But I must tell you that over the years I have recognised that LUCK is really spelt W-O-R-K. Things become attracted to you as you work towards your dreams. The more you focus on where you want to go the easier it becomes to achieve your goals. Starting small and working your way to bigger and bigger goals proves to yourself that you can achieve anything you put your mind to. The trick is to start working towards your goals immediately. Start taking action and don't stop! My goal is to raise your awareness of the potential and excellence that lies within you and to use it to help you achieve amazing things throughout your lifetime.

This is the book I wish I could have given myself when I was 20, just finishing university and starting in the work force. I would have told myself that I can do anything I set my mind to. Life can be fun, rewarding, exciting, filled with adventure and of course LOVE. I would have told myself that people around you are dealing with their own issues and one shouldn't get upset about small things. Plan on doing your personal bests (PBs) as often as you can and you will flourish.

My wish is that this book empowers thousands of women to seek more knowledge in their chosen wealth areas and to be kind to themselves and acknowledge that they are growing and doing the best they can. We are here to learn important life lessons and fulfill our individual purposes, so let your life energy flow and live your life to the best of your ability. Enjoy the journey and the legacy you are constantly building to leave behind for others to prosper from and enjoy.

May your life achievements make you immensely proud of what you have accomplished.

Sincerely,

Megan

How to use this book

If you're reading my book, there's a very good chance that you're looking for change in your life. To make sure you get the most benefit out of the information on every page, here's how I suggest you go about reading it:

Firstly, make a commitment to read the entire book from cover to cover and set a date by which you want to have it finished.

Buy yourself a journal, which we will call your Wealth Creation Journal (you'll learn more about this in Chapter 1).

Every chapter contains a series of exercises and questions that I strongly encourage you to complete as you go. You can complete the exercises in your Wealth Creation Journal, but I have also left space in the book if you'd prefer to write your answers there.

Finish every exercise in each chapter before moving onto the next if you really want to live an EXTRAORDINARY life! You may find that some of the exercises and actions you decide to take will challenge you and push you out of your comfort zone. This is a positive and very normal part of introducing changes to your life because it means you are growing and getting closer to the result you want. Push through these 'growing pains' and don't give up.

If you are having major relationship troubles, family issues, poor health, ongoing financial crises or other turmoil then you may feel that this book is too optimistic for you. I encourage you to make sure you are getting enough support, maybe therapy or counseling. KEEP READING. There may be simple techniques mentioned that help you shift your mindset so you understand that while things may not look like they are heading in the right direction in your life yet, there are tools you can use to plan and design your future. Keep looking forward at the great things that are possible in your life so that when times are tough you have a vision to keep you optimistic about your future.

If you have any questions as you go, please go to www.extraordinaryyou.net.

And finally, ENJOY YOURSELF! Learning should be a pleasure, not a chore, so get creative and have some fun!

CHAPTER 1

Wealth – What Does It Mean To You?

Extraordinary YOU

Ladies: grab a latte and turn off your mobile phone – we're going to have a chat. A chat about you – mother, mum-to-be, single woman, married woman, businesswoman, career woman.

Is your life everything you had hoped it would be? Do you have the home and the partner you'd dreamed of? Are your relationships with family and friends fulfilling? Do you have the job you wanted or the business you planned for? Are you taking that annual overseas holiday with family and friends? Are you feeling fulfilled and ALIVE?

If things aren't quite on track, don't worry - you've come to the right place; we can start from where you are now and take you to where you want to be.

Life really can be whatever you want it to be and you really can achieve anything you set your mind to if you choose to make it happen. Life is all about choice and nothing to do with luck or being dealt a good or bad hand. It takes work and there will be ups and downs along the way. But you can plan for, and work towards, fewer low times and more frequent and exciting 'up' times.

Your current situation is a direct result of the choices you have made so far. Of course there might be hands that you will be dealt that will put you outside what you consider to be 'normal'. But life has taught me that there is no such thing as 'normal'. Historically society has believed we have simple families of mum, dad and a couple of kids and everyone stays together, grows up and repeats the cycle. But now we

Chapter 1: Wealth – what does it mean to you?

know that picture is distorted. We have blended families and single parent families as well. We also have short and long term problems with finances, relationships and health affecting our lives. Do not get into the habit of thinking you need to fit into a stereotype. Understand that if something has happened to you that changed your direction in life like a divorce, you DO have opportunities to start again with new rules that YOU determine.

Saying that your life is the direct result of your choices might sound harsh if you're not living your dream life, but the good news is you can change it. Right at this minute you can choose to take responsibility for your life and make it everything you had ever dreamed. Or you can simply choose to continue to do what you've always done and continue to get the same results.

> 'If you keep doing what you've always done, you'll keep getting what you've always got.'
>
> ~ Jim Rohn ~

Taking responsibility for your life and deciding to make it extraordinary is probably one of the most important decisions you will make. Of course life will still happen around you; you still have to juggle a million things and not every day will be perfect. Once you understand that you are the creator of your life and you begin to introduce the strategies in this book, things will begin to change and you will start to see the magic unfold.

I'm here to tell you that your dreams CAN COME TRUE, but it's up to YOU.

Plan your attitude to life

It starts with a Positive Mental Attitude (PMA). This might sound too simplistic but the practice of choosing to have a positive spin on circumstances will begin your transformation towards an amazing life - as the old saying goes 'Turn lemons into lemonade'. Rather than spending time and energy focusing on what you don't like about a situation, use that time more wisely. Choose a positive outlook, and work towards solutions.

There are so many wonderful ideas and lessons to learn throughout this book, but unless you have an open mind and a PMA, you are probably going to miss out on a lot of it. Your attitude really can mean the difference between success and 'failure'. Don't worry though, think of failure as only a stepping stone or learning opportunity.

Make a decision now to keep your mind open to the new ideas that you will learn on the pages of this book and give things a go with a Positive Mental Attitude. You might just surprise yourself!

Your Wealth Creation Journal

Before we go too much further I want to introduce you to the idea of keeping a 'Wealth Creation Journal'. Buy a notebook/journal that you are proud of and will want to

Chapter 1: Wealth – what does it mean to you?

keep on hand. This journal is your best friend and tool on your way to becoming a more 'Extraordinary You'; it is where you will write your thoughts about:

- how you want to improve your future
- how you want to create wealth
- inspirational quotes that resonate for you
- training you have completed.

You can write about any personal development (self improvement) or thoughts that you come across or think about during your day. Make it a habit to write in this book everyday and use it as a reference when you need a pep talk or want to create something special in your life. Your journal will become a constant resource as you learn and grow.

Great leaders and teachers throughout history including Benjamin Franklin, Richard Branson and Jim Rohn have used a similar tool and most successful people I meet on my travels throughout the world do the same. I am never far from my journal; it really is a special book that I am constantly writing in and referring back to.

If you don't already have a journal you'd like to use, buy yourself one next time you're at the shops because you'll need it very soon!

What does 'wealth' mean to you?

Wealth is often on the top of the list when it comes to living your dream life. But wealth means something different to each of us. To some it means paying off the mortgage and living debt-free. While others see it as not having to worry about how to pay the gas and electricity bills and being able to pay for the kids' school excursions. To others it's absolute freedom to never work again and live in luxury with the best of everything.

I want you to think about wealth ladies, and what it really means to you.

Most of us have thought about having more money and in fact, it's something we probably think about almost every day. So what have you done about it? Have you:

1. Taken a few steps towards creating wealth but stopped when you got stuck on what to do next?
2. Pinned your hopes on winning the lottery or marrying a wealthy man? (I hope not!)
3. Given up because you don't believe that you could ever be wealthy?

Number 1 – If you answered yes, congratulations on getting started! If you're not sure what to do next or how to begin, keep reading, because this book is designed to help get you started and continue on your path to wealth. I will give you some simple action steps that will help you decide what to do

Chapter 1: Wealth – what does it mean to you?

and begin to achieve some small goals before moving onto bigger and bigger goals as your self-confidence grows.

Number 2 – If your wealth plan consists of marrying 'Mr Rich' or winning the lottery, it's time to get real and revise that plan quick smart. Believe me, there are no 'get rich quick schemes' that won't leave you with a giant headache and a long list of consequences. Creating your own wealth is up there among the most satisfying achievements in life. So no more waiting for something to just happen, you have to make it happen.

> 'A man is not a plan.'
>
> ~ Loral Langemeier ~

Number 3 – You don't believe you could ever be wealthy? Where did you get this belief? Did your parents struggle when you were growing up? Have you had some bad luck and now find yourself in difficult times? Believe me, most people struggle at some point in their lives; we all have our problems but with effort and a little education we can overcome these and prosper. The turnaround can start NOW. It may be an uphill climb at times but better that than a downhill spiral to a destination NO ONE wants to think about. Make a decision to start on your path to success now.

> 'Mistakes are stepping stones to success.'
>
> ~ Emily Dickinson ~

Real wealth

'Wealth' is often defined as having an abundance of money and/or material possessions of value. I have chosen to expand my definition of wealth to one that includes all areas of my life. Why? Because what's the point of having an abundance of money without people to share it with or the health to enjoy it? And why have so much money but not use it to help others?

As we begin our wealth creation journey together I invite you to consider expanding your definition of wealth to one that includes abundance in all areas of your life? I call this 'real wealth'.

To me, real wealth means having abundance in my family life, finances, social life, my environment, and spirituality. It also means living with less stress in my life and being able to let go of the small things that have no real impact on the big picture. As well as being proud of myself and what I have achieved.

Real wealth for me is the whole package and being able to balance the important things in life. What is 'real wealth' to you? From now on, when I refer to 'wealth', I am referring

Chapter 1: Wealth – what does it mean to you?

to this expanded, broader definition of wealth: plenty in all areas of your life that are significant to you.

> 'All money means to me is a pride in accomplishment.'
>
> ~ Ray Kroc ~

The secret to real wealth

One of the first and most important lessons I have learnt about becoming wealthy is that you need to work on yourself first. By this I mean understanding what drives and motivates you, controlling your self-talk and thoughts, choosing how and with whom you spend your time, learning how to communicate effectively with others and asking the right questions. One of the best ways to do this is to read.

When I first started in business I spent a lot of time working on myself and I still do. I read every personal development and wealth creation book I can get my hands on. At the end of each chapter, you will find a list of books that expand upon the themes and ideas of that chapter, so if something particularly resonates with you (or perhaps confuses you!) you can do some further research. I'd love you to read these books anyway, as I think they are amazing tools to help you on your way.

Start reading and as you find information you like, highlight the page it's on so you can refer back to it and write it in your Wealth Creation Journal. You might not particularly like everything you read and one book may resonate with you more than another, but one thing I can promise you is that even if you learn just one lesson from each book it will be worth it. Even one new piece of information could be worth thousands, hundreds of thousands or even millions of dollars to you – so keep reading!

> 'There is only one corner of the universe you can be certain of improving, and that's your own self.'
>
> ~ Aldous Huxley ~

What do you think about yourself?

As you begin your personal development journey, you will start to discover a lot about yourself including what you believe you're capable of and what you think of yourself. Much of what you uncover may surprise you because many of our beliefs are subconscious, or unconscious, which means you generally aren't aware of them and you definitely will be surprised at how much of an impact these beliefs can have on the choices you make in life.

I want you to ask yourself the following two questions, and be very honest with your answers. Write the questions and answers in your Wealth Creation Journal and mark it with today's date.

Chapter 1: Wealth – what does it mean to you?

Do you believe you could be wealthy in all areas of your life?

_____

_____

_____

_____

Do you think you are capable of creating your own wealth?

_____

_____

_____

_____

If you answered no to either or both of these questions or if your answer was uncertain, hesitant or full of 'buts', 'ifs' or 'maybes', don't worry; this is simply your starting point. We just need to get to work on building your self-belief because, if you don't believe you can be wealthy or that you're capable of creating wealth, you risk sabotaging your hard work or losing your wealth once you have it.

Let's get to work on your self-belief. In your Wealth Creation Journal, I want you to write down a small goal. Your goal could be to finish reading this book in 14 days. As you finish each chapter consider it a small win towards your goal and notice how you feel. Each step towards achieving your goal adds to your self-belief and what you believe you are capable of. Once you achieve your first goal set another and watch your self-belief grow. Each time you set a goal make it a bit more challenging than the last. We will talk about goal setting in more detail in Chapter 2.

You are totally awesome!

Turn to a new page in your Wealth Creation Journal and at the top of the page write 'I am awesome!' Underneath that heading, write down everything you have accomplished in your life that you are proud of and any positive feedback and comments you have received. Don't hold back!

Your list might include:
- I took part in the high school debating competition
- I was voted school prefect
- I finished high school
- I graduated from university
- I was told I had nice eyes
- I gave birth to two beautiful children
- I paid cash for my first car
- I paid off my credit card

Chapter 1: Wealth – what does it mean to you?

- I maintained my goal weight for 12 months
- I learned to meditate
- I bought an investment property
- I got a promotion at work
- I won employee of the month
- I knitted a scarf
- I grew a tomato plant and now use fresh tomatoes in my cooking
- I cook the best lasagne in town
- I read five personal development books.

And the list will go on…

I want you to keep adding to this list, so make sure you leave plenty of space in your journal (even a couple of pages), and then anytime you feel a little down or lost and need a boost, get your Wealth Creation Journal out and remind yourself just how awesome you really are!

It's easy to forget what you have achieved and it's important to always remind yourself exactly how far you have come. You need to be your own cheerleader and continuously promote yourself to yourself.

How will you look after yourself when you retire?

Ladies, just as an aside, what are you doing to ensure you can pay for your OWN retirement? Statistics in Australia suggest that 40 per cent of marriages will end in divorce, with similar statistics in New Zealand and higher in the US, that around 20 per cent of families are single parent families, that a large percentage of women are supporting older parents and women out-live their partners by an average of five years. Taking all of this into consideration means that we MUST be self-sufficient. Do you know ANYONE who can live comfortably on the government provided pension? Do you think the pension is going to be there for you as a secure safety net? Most families cannot comfortably live on one income anymore.

You may not have the vision to be WEALTHY but you MUST have the plan to fully support yourself and your dependants. As you go through the questions in this chapter, make sure you consider the minimum level of wealth to sustain your life. Whatever plans you set for yourself, the most important thing is to start NOW!

Who are you spending time with?

Your self-belief or lack of self-belief may have been built on the opinion of others. If you spend time with negative people and people who criticise you and your ideas, it's time to start choosing more carefully the people you spend time

Chapter 1: Wealth – what does it mean to you?

with. You might have heard the Jim Rohn quote that, 'You are the average of the five people you spend the most time with.'

Who are you spending time with?

_____

_____

_____

_____

_____

It's not always easy to separate yourself from people who are negative or critical of you. You don't have to banish them from your life, just spend less time with them and when you do see them, have a few strategies up your sleeve to change the topic or simply ignore the negative talk. Being aware of how you feel when you are around negative people helps you manage the situation. Don't let yourself be pulled into the conversation and find yourself agreeing. Sometimes, you may just have a nagging sense of feeling worse about yourself, your family or your life after you've spent time with someone or a particular group. Don't ignore it! Try to take yourself away from this situation and think quietly about it: what made you feel that way? Did someone say or do something that made you feel that way? Start trusting your intuition about the people around you and the situations you enter into.

It is a great idea to start purposefully going to events attended by like-minded people. Consider networking events or personal development seminars – you will generally find the people at these seminars want to improve their lives and achieve goals and will be on the same wealth creation path as you.

How are you spending your time?

Along with thinking about the people you spend time with, you also need to think about how <u>you</u> spend your time.

To build your confidence and create an extraordinary life, you need to spend your time wisely, doing things that will contribute to your personal growth and your bank balance, such as producing products to sell or making a sales call. I choose not to watch much television because I don't find it to be very uplifting and positive. I would prefer to go for a walk on the beach, play outside with my children, read a book, work on my business, exercise or attend an educational seminar. If I do watch television I carefully choose what I watch to make sure I am either going to learn something, be informed or feel inspired or laugh because I believe these things add to my life, while a lot of tv-watching is just time lost and it can sometimes be downright negative.

It's very important to make conscious decisions about what you put into your mind. If you are watching and listening to rubbish, you can't expect your mind to produce anything other than rubbish. You might have heard the saying, 'Garbage in, garbage out'.

Chapter 1: Wealth – what does it mean to you?

Of course it doesn't mean you can't ever just chill out and watch a bit of fun tv with the kids: I just don't recommend that you spend hours at it daily.

What are you passionate about?

Have you ever noticed that when you're doing something you love you lose track of time and have endless energy? Take notice when this happens because whatever you're doing might well be your passion.

If you haven't yet found your passion, my advice is to stop worrying and start doing. Once you start doing the things in life that you've always wanted to do you will soon discover what makes you truly happy and how you can make a difference on this planet. And this will be different for everyone, but I promise you that once you have found something you are passionate about, you will be driven with more excitement, enjoyment and enthusiasm than you can ever imagine. You will wake up in the morning with energy, drive and excitement to work on your goals. The more passion and excitement you have the more you will get done every day, and the more you will get out of life.

I still remember the exact moment that I discovered my passion. Fresh out of university and working in a bank at just 22 years old, I was assigned a couple of team members who were quite a few years older than me. During the annual review with one of my team members, it became obvious that her reduced work output was due to depression and not being able to change her situation. I was young and unworldly so I dared not give advice but I had just finished reading *The Magic of Thinking Big* by David Schwartz and decided to give the book to her in the hope she would find some helpful information. The very next week at work she returned the book and said, 'Thank you, I really LOVED it and I wrote my goals just like the book said'. Two weeks later she came into work with a HUGE bunch of flowers for me and said: 'You changed my life. My goal was to earn enough money to pay my son's credit card while he travels overseas because he has run out of money, to repay the bank loan I needed for my divorce and to pay my ex-husband's gambling debts. Last night I won $100,000 in the lottery so I am now able to help my son, pay off my loan and have a nice sum left over towards a house deposit.' TRUE STORY!

It was in that very moment that I realised my passion for teaching people about personal development and how to achieve their goals. It is extremely rewarding and has forced me to live a life of continued learning. I am always seeking out books, audio CDs and teachers and put their methods into practice.

It was some years later in the mid 1990s while doing a Stephen R. Covey (author of *The 7 Habits of Highly Effective People*) course that I discovered my life's purpose. We were given the time to write down what was important to us. Never before had I really taken the time to sit quietly and think about what was important to me. I realised that my purpose was: 'To leave the world a better place because of my actions.'

Chapter 1: Wealth – what does it mean to you?

I keep my purpose short and non-specific because it can guide me in any situation and allows me to think about what action will result in the greatest outcome.

Take some time to sit quietly and write down in your Wealth Creation Journal what is important to you. You might just discover your purpose in life. For example, your purpose might be to be a wonderful mother; to be an inspiring teacher dedicated to making every child in your class feel valued and special; to connect with and inspire others; to help others; to produce music that people love and that makes them feel great; to provide a product or service that makes a difference.

_____

_____

_____

> 'The work of your life is to discover your purpose and get on with the business of living it.'
>
> ~ Oprah Winfrey ~

What drives you to succeed?

If you've ever had an 'a-ha' moment, I'm sure you can remember exactly where you were and who you were with. I have had many 'a-ha' moments throughout my life, but I wanted to share with you a story from one of my friends.

She was catching up with a colleague of hers who also happens to be a life coach and as always their conversation quickly turned to business and self-development. He started asking her about her values and at this stage she wasn't really sure what they were. So he kept asking her what she valued and every time she gave him an answer he would ask, 'Why?' This went on and on until the answers kept coming back to the same three responses; freedom, family and love and these, he said, were her highest values. He then explained to her that everything we do in life and every decision we make is driven by these values. For instance, if my friend was to go shopping she would make a beeline to the bookshop and could spend hours there instead of the shoe shops because when she reads, she learns and when she learns she is growing as a person and businesswoman, which in turn increases her income and gives her greater freedom, which is one of her highest values! My friend was so excited to discover her highest values and said for the first time in her life she understood why she put so much energy into certain activities, and loved it, but procrastinated on other tasks. It was a huge 'a-ha' moment for her.

Knowing your highest values helps you to understand your choices and behaviours, and will assist you to understand

Chapter 1: Wealth – what does it mean to you?

exactly why you are in your current position. For example, you want more money but as fast as it comes in the door it's going out the door. If this is your experience, it might be that as much as you think you want more money, wealth just isn't one of your highest values and until it becomes one of your top values your situation just isn't going to change. Let's take health as another example. If you eat well and exercise regularly, it's likely that health is one of your highest values. If, on the other hand, you smoke, drink heavily, don't exercise and eat junk food most days, health probably isn't one of your highest values and every diet you attempt will continue to fail.

Later in the book we will talk about self-esteem and self-worth and the affect they have on your ability to achieve the level of success you desire. They play a big role in addition to your values.

One of the best methods I have come across to work out your highest values is the Demartini Value Determination Process®. Developed by personal development leader Dr John Demartini, the process involves answering 13 simple questions about your life. Let's work through it together now.

Take out your Wealth Creation Journal and on a page titled 'My Values' write down the following questions, leaving space under each one for your answers.

- How do you fill your personal space?
- How do you spend your time?
- How do you spend your energy?

- How do you spend your money?
- Where do you have the most order and organisation?
- Where are you most reliable, disciplined or focused?
- What do you think about, and what is your most dominant thought?
- What do you visualise and realise?
- What is your internal dialogue?
- What do you talk about in social settings?
- What inspires you?
- What are the most consistent long-term goals that inspire you?
- What do you love to learn and read about the most?

Under each question write a list of things that are important to you. When you have finished, look over your answers and take notice of any repetition in your answers. You might notice that 'family' comes up a number of times, as well as 'money' and then 'fun' perhaps. Write down the top three words or activities that occur the most and these are probably your highest values.

When you discover your values, you will understand why you procrastinate on certain tasks, why others are easy, how you make decisions and why you've reached your current position in life.

Chapter 1: Wealth – what does it mean to you?

Examples of common values are:

- Health
- Love
- Wealth
- Happiness
- Comfort
- Security
- Adventure
- Learning
- Peace
- Intimacy
- Fun
- Trustworthiness
- Freedom
- Accomplishment
- Charity.

For more information on the Demartini Value Determination Process® visit www.drdemartini.com/value_determination

> 'No person is committed to anything but the fulfillment of their highest values.'
>
> ~ Dr John F. Demartini ~

How can I change my values?

Once you've discovered your highest values, you may decide that you want to change them so they align with your goals. Values organically change throughout our lives anyway, when a significant life event occurs (having a baby, a death of a loved one etc), when you gain insights, when you start spending time with different people etc. So wanting to change your values is perfectly fine – you're really just going to speed up a natural process.

To change your values, or elevate a value that is lower on your list of values, you need to think about your future and ideally how you will be living your life (see Chapter 2 for detailed exercises on how to do this). When you read your goals, think about the values you will need to accomplish them. For example, if you have a goal to improve your health and fitness, the value that will need to be a priority for you will be 'health', 'fitness' or 'self-discipline'. If your goal is financial freedom the value you will need might be 'wealth' or 'security'.

I will share with you Dr Demartini's method to change or elevate goals. It does require a lot of focus and commitment, so I suggest setting aside a good hour for this and not giving up half way through if you really want this change. Start by writing down the value you want to elevate to your top three. Let's say it's wealth. You then need to link wealth back to your existing top three values 200 times. We'll stick with our earlier example and use 'freedom', 'love' and 'family'. Ask yourself, 'How does having more money (or wealth) give me

Chapter 1: Wealth – what does it mean to you?

more freedom?' and 'How does having more money give me more fun?', and 'How does having more money give me more time with my family?'. Keep asking these questions over and over until you have 200 answers. If you stick with this exercise and come up with the 200 reasons, it is highly effective and the value you want to elevate should now be up there in the top three.

If you find it too hard, you might need a one-on-one session with someone trained as an NLP Master Certified Practitioner who can take you through the values-changing exercise.

Women and wealth

Did you know women in Australia make approximately 80 per cent of the household spending decisions? Similar numbers in the USA mean that women of the US have a purchasing power of more than US$5 trillion (more than the economy of Japan in 2008). We are moving into a knowledge-based economy that depends more on solving problems and less on physical strength. Therefore it rewards smarts; women now equal or exceed the education levels of men in numerous countries. Don't worry if you don't have a great education. Women naturally know how to solve problems and this gives them the perfect skills necessary to start their own businesses. The growth of the entire global economy over the past two decades has much more to do with the increase in female employment in the developed world than new technology or the growth of China and India. But with this growth women are demanding flexibility in the work place. This is to your advantage my friend!

> In general, money means security for women and freedom to men. Every day 400 US women start their own businesses, twice the rate of US men. Clearly the reason for this is that women are taking control of their financial futures. What about you? Do you want to be secure in your future?

What are you thankful for?

Think about a typical day in your life. It's crazy, busy right? Between getting the kids ready for school, feeding the pets, trying to fit in a conversation with your partner, organising the household, a visit to the gym and working, it can all get a little too much. And if one thing goes wrong, the entire day tends to spiral in that same direction.

Your whole life would be better if only you had five minutes to just stop and relax, if only the kids would just make their beds or feed the dog, if only your partner could cook and help out with the dishes, or if only you weren't single or got that promotion last year. Sound familiar?

It's easy to feel overwhelmed and stay focused on what's going wrong or what you haven't got when you live a busy life or you're not particularly happy. But let's get real here and flip all this negativity on its head.

What could happen if you focused on the good things in your life and the things that are working well? How would that feel?

Chapter 1: Wealth – what does it mean to you?

Think of just one thing right now that you're thankful for and write it in your Wealth Creation Journal. Even if it's as simple as being thankful to the person who stood up and gave you their seat on the train, or being grateful to the driver who slowed down so you could move into the turning lane in peak hour traffic, or the work colleague who made you a cup of tea at the office.

How about next time your children don't make their beds, you let go of the frustration and be thankful that you have healthy children who are so busy having fun they forgot to make their beds? And the next time your partner forgets to tell you he's going to be home late, be thankful when he gets home that he's safe and well. This is not to say you are letting them off the hook but is merely changing the way you feel about it.

Gratitude is one of the simplest yet most profound exercises we can master on our wealth creation journey. You see ladies, what we put out into the world is what we get back. So if you are cranky and angry all the time and focused on what's lacking in your life, you're going to keep on attracting the same thing. It's called the Law of Attraction – what you give out is what you get back.

If you focus on the positive things in your life, guess what? You're going to attract more of these great experiences. You will also find that there is so much in your life to be grateful for that you feel happier and more content than when you focused on what was wrong.

Grab your Wealth Creation Journal and start writing a list of what you're grateful for. If it's difficult at first to think of anything, here are a few ideas to get you started:

- Thank you for my great health and energy
- I give thanks for the beautiful sunny day
- Thank you for the clean water we have to drink
- I am so grateful that I have the ability to read this book
- I am so grateful I have clothes to wear
- I am so thankful to have two healthy, gorgeous children
- I am so excited to be planning our next vacation
- I am glad I have friends who make me laugh
- My book club fills me with joy
- I am grateful for the unconditional love that my cat and dog show me.

_____

_____

_____

_____

Chapter 1: Wealth – what does it mean to you?

Start small if you need to. Notice how good you feel as you write and start to think about the wonderful things in your life from the small things to the really significant things. Life is looking pretty good isn't it?

Entire books have been written on the power of gratitude because it really can change your life. A great habit to develop is writing a list of what you're grateful for everyday. Set aside five minutes when you wake up or just before you go to sleep to write down what you're grateful for and watch as even more wonderful things come into your life.

Growing pains

When I first moved to the States with my husband and started to invest in property, oil and gas and began to learn about network marketing, I was nervous. This was so new to me - all of it. I was used to a steady job and a regular income but now here I was in a foreign country taking risks with our money and not knowing what the outcome would be. I was way out of my comfort zone.

As you read this book and start to implement changes and take action you are going to feel nervous, scared and challenged too. You are going to want to put the book down and go back to your comfort level. Or you may read to the end but not want to do any of the exercises.

Trust me ladies, these feelings are normal and all part of change. Learn to see the good side of change and notice how your situation improves as you take small steps towards 'Real Wealth'.

If you want to change your life, you need to accept that you're going to go through periods of feeling uncomfortable. Think of it as having 'growing pains' and I promise you that if you push through the fear and don't give up it will be well worth it.

> 'If you want to conquer fear, don't sit home and think about it. Go out and get busy.'
>
> ~ Dale Carnegie ~

Action Plan

As you read each chapter, make sure you take the time to answer the questions on the 'Action Plan' page before you move to the next chapter. These answers are important and will develop as you keep your mind active and on task towards taking control of your life. A good place to write your answers is in your Wealth Creation Journal for easy reference.

What does real wealth mean to you?

Does it mean:

- lots of money?
- happy family?
- spiritual abundance?
- mega health?

Chapter 1: Wealth – what does it mean to you?

- true love
- immense joy and happiness?
- incredible relationships?
- continual learning?
- exciting career?
- supporting lots of charities?
- time to create beautiful things – leave a legacy?
- seizing every moment?
- something else?

_____

_____

_____

_____

What traits do you most admire in people you consider to be wealthy?

_____

_____

_____

_____

What motivates you to achieve this real wealth?

_____

_____

_____

_____

What are you prepared to do to work towards your real wealth?

_____

_____

_____

_____

What are you passionate about?

_____

_____

_____

_____

Chapter 1: Wealth – what does it mean to you?

What is your life's purpose?

_____

_____

_____

_____

What relationships in your life make you happy?

_____

_____

_____

_____

_____

Recommended reading

Think and Grow Rich, Napoleon Hill

Creating Affluence – the A to Z steps to a richer life, Deepak Chopra

You Inc, John McGrath

The Secret, Rhonda Byrne

Count your Blessings: The Healing Power of Gratitude and Love, Dr. John F. Demartini

Like a Virgin – Secrets they won't teach you at business school, Sir Richard Branson

CHAPTER 2

It's Time To Dream

> 'If you don't design your own life plan, chances are you'll fall into someone else's plan. And guess what they have planned for you? Not much.'
>
> ~ Jim Rohn ~

Right ladies, it's time to start creating this amazing life of yours. If you could be, do and have anything you wanted, do you know what your life would look like? Do you have a clear vision of it? We often limit ourselves because we don't believe our wildest dreams could ever really come true. We think that others are better than we are and that they can achieve their dream but we can't. At the end of the day, we are all created the same way biologically and we're all going to end up exactly the same when our life ends. So why then can someone else achieve their dreams but you doubt yourself?

I'm here to tell you that you absolutely <u>can</u> achieve everything you want if you're willing to take action, stay focused and never give up! So let's have some fun and <u>dream big.</u>

Imagine if you were to take a 30-day all expenses paid working holiday on your private jet (of course!). In the space below or in your Wealth Creation Journal, answer the following questions to really paint an amazing picture in your mind: Where would you go on your private jet? Who would you take with you? What would you do? What adventures would you have? What awards would you win? Who would you meet?

Chapter 2: It's Time To Dream

Who would you help? What would you buy? What would you create? How would you feel? What would you learn and discover? Get creative ladies – this is the trip of a lifetime!

_____

_____

_____

_____

_____

_____

The point of this exercise is to allow yourself to dream a BIG dream. You don't want mediocre. You want amazing, out-of-this world dreams. Remember, we are all created the same and all end up the same, so you are just as deserving and capable of creating your dream life as the next person, but now you are learning skills and gaining tools to help you get there.

Once you start achieving this level of success that sees you taking these incredible, all-expenses paid holidays (or living the lifestyle according to your own definition of success), everyday life is going to look very different to the way it looks now. So before you forget life as you now know it, write down what a typical day looks like for you right now. It's a good idea to put the date on this too.

_____

_____

_____

_____

_____

_____

Now create your ultimate, typical day. Would you enjoy some early morning exercise before sitting down to breakfast with your family? Once the children are at school, would you write some of your book before meeting friends for lunch? Give a speech in your chosen profession after lunch then enjoy picking up the kids and watching them enjoy sport or music or some other activity before heading home to a beautiful home cooked meal and a family games night with close friends and their kids? Oh wait! That's mine. What is yours? Remember; don't hold back, make it **BIG**.

_____

_____

_____

Chapter 2: It's Time To Dream

_____

_____

_____

_____

_____

Don't underestimate the importance of completing this exercise and what it can do to your mindset. Give it a go! Let your imagination run wild and be ambitious. Oh, and remember to think happy thoughts and smile while you're creating your amazing life on paper! Be ambitious in what you are asking for.

Sometimes we achieve substantial successes but, because we forget where we came from, we don't celebrate, acknowledge and have gratitude for this success. This can keep you feeling stuck even when you are not. Taking note of where you are, where you want to be and what you do to get there will help you become aware and acknowledge yourself - because somebody's got to, and it may as well be you!

> 'The future belongs to those who believe in the beauty of their dreams.'
>
> ~ Eleanor Roosevelt ~

What does freedom mean to you?

While you're in the creative groove, let's talk about freedom: what does that word mean to you? What choices do you want to be free to make? How do you define 'financial freedom'?

I have spoken to many people who tell me they want financial freedom but when I ask them what that means, they don't really know. Let's be clear: everyone's definition will vary but if you want financial freedom, you need to know exactly what it means to you and then be able to put a dollar figure on that (or maybe a series of dollar figures). My definition of financial freedom is being free from financial worries and being able to choose how I live my life without financial restriction. I know exactly how much money I need to earn every month to live according to this definition.

To start with, you might define financial freedom as having enough money to cover your financial commitments and any other important or fun costs that come up - such as school excursions, a special romantic weekend away or an overseas adventure - without any stress. This might mean that you need to earn $70,000 a year, for example. A few years down the track, you might redefine financial freedom and aim for $200,000 a year or $1,000,000 a year.

So, what does financial freedom mean to you? I really encourage you to complete this exercise and all of the exercises in this book, because they aim to help you get focused and clear about what you want in your life – they will set your direction! Many people live life with no real

Chapter 2: It's Time To Dream

direction or goals, and wonder why they are not satisfied. It's like catching a bus: you need to know where you are going and which bus will take you there, otherwise you don't know where you will end up, or you stay standing on the platform while everyone passes you by. If you're serious about creating your dream life, do yourself a favour and complete each exercise.

Financial freedom means ...

_____

_____

_____

_____

_____

_____

_____

> ' The fulfillment of your dream lies with YOU. Once you realise this, nothing will stop you.'
>
> ~ Megan Wolfenden ~

Where are you heading?

You should be getting a clearer picture now of the things and experiences that will make your life exciting and fulfilling. Isn't it good to have clarity?

The next step is to turn your dreams into goals. One of the common practices of all successful people is having their goals written down. So you guessed it, if you're going to be successful you need to start writing!

I learned the power of writing down my goals in 2006. In January of that year my husband Anthony and I attended a three-day course with Robert Kiyosaki's mentor Jayne Johnson while we were in Phoenix, Arizona. It was a great weekend of personal development focusing on our mindset, self-worth and making sure we believed that we deserved success. On the Saturday night of that weekend we were given the homework of writing down 12 goals we wanted to achieve. Anthony and I quickly wrote down some goals that night without putting too much thought or effort into the exercise. The next day, however, we were instructed to spend hours on those goals and installing all of this emotion around them. We were a little annoyed with the whole exercise because it was very right-brained (creative, intuitive, feelings, subconscious) and we are such left-brained (logical) people; we wanted action plans and 30, 60 and 90-days goals. Consequently, after the course we just put the goals in a drawer and forgot about them. In March 2007 I found those goals and was in a state of absolute disbelief when I realised that many of my goals had happened as planned. We had not understood the value of the course until then.

Chapter 2: It's Time To Dream

My first goal read 'By December 2006, I will be earning $60,000 in passive income per month.'

And would you believe that in December 2006, we had earned the exact amount of passive income I had written in that goal. I became a massive believer in goal setting from that moment on!

A friend of mine had a similar experience with goal setting. She had decided she wanted to leave her government job to work for herself. She wrote her goal in a journal that she kept in her bedside drawer.

'By June 2010 I will be working full-time in my own business.'

In the meantime she got to work starting her own small business from home, working at night when she got home from her government job, and on weekends. Two years later in September 2010, she was unpacking boxes after having just moved house, when she came across her journal. She had completely forgotten that she'd written that goal and her face lit up with the biggest smile because three months earlier in June 2010 she had quit her government job and started working full-time for herself.

Never underestimate the power of a written goal. They give you clarity around what you want and when you want it.

I'm going to introduce you to the SMART goal system, but you can use any system that works for you – the most important aspect of this is that you have something written down.

A SMART goal is:
S – Specific
M – Measurable
A – Action-oriented
R – Realistic
T – Time Bound

For example:
It's 13 June 2016 and I am sitting in the media room of my dream home at 22 Awesome Street, Brisbane, Australia. My family is with me and we are so happy and comfortable in our new four-bedroom home.

or

It's now 10 January 2015, and I have just logged into my bank account and the balance is $100,000. I feel so relieved, satisfied and proud!

Write one goal that you'd like to achieve in the next three or six months. Don't get bogged down with the wording of your goal though. Just get it written down. Make sure it's something that you really want and that you're passionate about, and something that will have a massive impact on your life when you finally do get it. Remember, we're dreaming big, out-of-this-world dreams!

_____

_____

_____

Chapter 2: It's Time To Dream

_____

_____

_____

_____

_____

_____

One of the pioneers of personal development, Earl Nightingale shares a wonderful idea in his audio *The Strangest Secret*. Earl suggests taking a blank piece of card that will fit in your purse or wallet. On one side write your goal, very clearly and precisely, and on the other write these words from the Sermon on the Mount (Matthew 7:7):

'Ask and it shall be given you,
Seek and you shall find,
Knock and it shall be opened unto you.'

Keep the card in your purse or wallet and read it several times every day.

Keeping your goals clearly in your mind is an important part of goal setting.

Get clear about future goals

Once your first goal is written down it's time to think about what else you want. Because once you've achieved your first goal you're going to need another goal to focus on to ensure you keep moving towards more success. Recently I was talking to a businesswoman at a seminar who was telling me that some years ago after achieving her goal of building her dream house she mentally hit rock bottom. Despite having a magnificent house to live in she felt lost and depressed and couldn't work out why. After thinking about her life for a few weeks, she realised that she had no goals planned that she could work towards. She'd achieved her 'big, beautiful house' goal but didn't know what her next focus was. From that point on, she has always had a new goal to start working on once one was achieved. That's not to say you shouldn't stop and enjoy your achievements, but know that you will need to seek new challenges to keep growing.

Schedule time in your diary in the next week to write out the goals you will focus on once you achieved your first goal. You might want to set some mutual goals with your partner too, so you'll need to make time together to do that. I know couples who plan a weekend away to a resort where they can't be interrupted and spend the weekend brainstorming the next 12 months and beyond together, writing their mutual goals down.

Start with the end in mind

While my initial experience with goal setting was to write the goal and put it away and forget about it, it's not the way I have

Chapter 2: It's Time To Dream

done things since. After that first experience, I kept my goals in a place in my office where I could see them regularly. I consistently and persistently focused on my huge goals in order to achieve huge success.

I let go of the need to meet the goal at exactly the date I set, because I realised that while it's essential to set a date so that you stay motivated and focused, it's more important to know what you WANT to achieve. I have missed many dates set to achieve my goals, and I am okay with that. I simply reassess the goal and the timeline, adjust my action steps and keep going. I have also achieved things that I had on my vision board (refer to page 61 for how to create your vision board) without them being in writing and without a deadline. The most important thing is that my subconscious knows what I am working towards and I am content to keep working on important activities that help me achieve desired outcomes.

You need to see your goal as much as possible to remain clear about what you want and to keep heading in the right direction. But of course, no goal can be achieved without taking <u>action</u>. The next step on this exciting journey is to work out what actions you're going to take to achieve your goal. We're going to start with the end in mind and plan what actions you need to take to get there.

Let's use my example of wanting to achieve $60,000 passive income per month by December 2006. Now at the time of writing that goal I had absolutely no idea how we were going to achieve it, but two months after setting that goal and locking it in our subconscious by writing it in Australian dollars, US Dollars and ounces of gold, we attended another Robert Kiyosaki event. At each break during the weekend we moved tables to meet different people and network. During one session I sat next to a lovely woman who was clearly an astute businesswoman and she introduced me to a business opportunity with a network marketing company.

It really caught my attention and I continued to research it and test the products with family and friends. I was hesitant to get involved in network marketing but the products were amazing and the numbers added up. When we came back to Australia in March, we decided to launch the business here and started networking, writing and implementing a marketing plan, building a website, running events and doing everything we could think of to make our business a success. We started attracting clients and other like-minded people who wanted to do what we were doing!

Things really started to take off and we stayed focused on growing the business and learning as much as we could about business and our products. We regularly took international trips to study and learn from others in our organisation, and even started speaking at events to share our story.

We loved the product and the business and remained absolutely focused on achieving huge success.

Within no time it was December 2006 and we were earning a great income and working hard. By March I found the goal we had written and was amazed and exhilarated that we had achieved it.

Chapter 2: It's Time To Dream

So you can see that achieving my goal took massive action, focus and commitment. We were also driven, passionate and excited, which was a HUGE part of our success.

With your end goal in mind, I want you to write down what actions you're going to take to get there.

In your Wealth Creation Journal, or on the lines below complete the following exercise.

Goal:

_____

_____

_____

Action 1:

_____

_____

_____

Date to be achieved by: _____

Action 2:

_____

_____

_____

Date to be achieved by: _____

Action 3:

_____

_____

_____

Date to be achieved by: _____

Action 4:

_____

_____

_____

Date to be achieved by: _____

Chapter 2: It's Time To Dream

Action 5:

_____

_____

_____

Date to be achieved by: _____

Keep writing actions until you think you've exhausted all activities to achieve your goal and then start! If you really set your mind to it, you'll be amazed what you will achieve in the next 30, 60 and 90 days.

Each day take baby steps to achieve each action item. You will be amazed at how 30-plus consecutive days of working on important tasks towards a goal really does reap results.

And remember to enjoy the journey and what you learn along the way, because this is just as important.

> 'Never leave the site of a goal without first taking some form of positive action towards its attainment.'
>
> ~ Anthony Robbins ~

No more excuses

Have you already started coming up with excuses about why you're not going to start work on your goals or complete the exercises in the book? Or have you decided that perhaps you're best to wait until your youngest child has started school, you've had your holiday, or you've finished the next load of washing before you begin working on your personal development and wealth creation?

We're all busy and sometimes it would be so much easier to just chill out on the couch and watch the latest reality show instead of working on your goals and wealth creation strategies. However, if you don't start today, you'll likely put it off tomorrow and the next day and so on. And then in 12 months time you'll still be doing exactly what you're doing today. You're probably reading this book because you want something different, so NOW is the time to start. There is never going to be the perfect time, because you've probably noticed that you always have something that needs doing!

Once you're clear on your current goals, the next key ingredient is to take action. What is the first thing you are going to do? It may be that you're going to complete the action steps from the previous exercise. Write it down now:

_____

_____

_____

Chapter 2: It's Time To Dream

Now set the date and time (in the next few days) that you are going to take this action.

_____

Procrastination

If you find that you're procrastinating and doing anything in sight to avoid starting work on your goals, it might be that you need to adjust the goal to be more aligned with what you really want. Or maybe the goal isn't really the one you want to focus on right now and you just need to choose another one to work towards. Perhaps some fear is coming up; fear of failure or fear of success. Remember that this is all new to you so it's normal to feel nervous, scared and challenged. The key here is to take one step at a time and not to let these feelings beat you. You're experiencing 'growing pains' (refer to Chapter 1) and it's all part of making your life 'extraordinary'.

When it comes to finding the impetus for making a start, remember this adage:

> 'Don't wait. The time is never going to be just right.'
>
> ~ Napoleon Hill ~

If you are afraid of success OR failure remember this:

> 'What I know for sure: Fear comes from uncertainty. Once you clarify your purpose for doing something, the way to do it becomes clear.'
>
> ~ Oprah Winfrey ~

See yourself living an extraordinary life

Get into a comfortable position on the lounge, at your desk or in bed – wherever is most convenient for you. Close your eyes, take some deeps breaths, and as you do this start to see yourself in this picture: 'You've dropped the kids at school, or you have the day off work, and you've finished your morning jobs and have cleared your schedule for an hour or two. You don't have to be anywhere in a hurry so you decide to go to your favourite café. The best seat in the house is free and as you sit down the waiter comes over to take your order and have a chat. You sit back, relax and just allow yourself to take a few breaths and collect your thoughts after another busy start to the day.' This is YOUR time now so stay in this picture for as long as you like.

As you visualise yourself at the café, sipping your drink of choice, notice how you feel and what you see. When you're ready to leave the café, come back to this page and we'll have a chat.

Chapter 2: It's Time To Dream

Congratulations for taking some time out for yourself and putting your imagination to work. How did you feel when you were visualising yourself at the cafe? Were you relaxed? What café were you at? What were you drinking? Where were you sitting? Did you notice what you were wearing and what the waiter looked like? Was the café busy, or did you have the whole place to yourself?

Visualisation is one the most important skills for creating your dream life, and if you could see yourself at the café, then you have successfully visualised!

Throughout my journey of creating real wealth, I have learned time and again from industry leaders and my own experience that you must be able to see in your mind what you want to hold in your hands. And I don't just mean that you imagine it once and move on, expecting that it will arrive on your doorstep the next day. I mean really seeing it and seeing it often so that you remain completely focused on your desire.

There are a number of theories about why visualising helps to manifest the experience into your life. Quantum physics suggests that when you think about what you want and see it in your mind's eye you are energetically attracting it.

Another theory suggests that our subconscious mind is unable to separate what's real from what's in our imagination. So the more we visualise what we want, the more our minds believe it to be happening.

Elite athletes visualise the entire race from stepping onto the starting block and hearing the noise of the crowd, to touching the wall at the end of the pool, or crossing the finishing line on the track, many times before the actual race. Effectively, this visualisation is training the mind to enhance their performance and get used to having the experience they are working so hard towards. This is now a widely accepted tool for enhancing performance and there have been numerous studies citing its efficacy: you can use it too!

Visualisation is a powerful tool, so let's put your imagination to work on turning your dreams into reality.

There are a variety of tools and methods you can use to visualise your goals and dream life. I mentioned I like to use vision boards and write SMART goals. The techniques you decide to use are completely up to you, but you must use at least one method and use it regularly. You might even like to try a variety of techniques and then continue to use the ones you enjoy and find to be effective for you.

> 'Imagination is everything. It is the preview of life's coming attractions.'
>
> ~ Albert Einstein ~

Chapter 2: It's Time To Dream

Create your own vision board

Every year or so I create what is called a vision board, or dream board that is filled with pictures, words and images of the things I want to achieve. Throughout the year I collect pictures of experiences I want to have and things I want to own, the goals I want to achieve and words that mean something to me; it might be a holiday destination, a beautiful healthy meal, a peaceful setting or words such as 'write', 'passion' or 'leave a legacy'. Sometimes I look for specific pictures like a photo of a polar bear (I want to take my family to visit them soon) and a raised vegetable garden that I want to build in my backyard. I built the raised vegetable garden this year and am on to my second harvest of fruit, vegetables and herbs. The best part is that I didn't have space at my house when I set that goal but we have since bought and moved into a house with plenty of space for a veggie garden. I knew exactly where it would go when we bought the house.

I set aside time at the end of the year or at the beginning of the New Year, and cut out the pictures and words from magazines and brochures and paste them onto cardboard to create a collage of the experiences that I want to have in my life. I laminate the board and hang it in my office where I can see it everyday. Looking at my vision board makes me feel happy and excited about working towards my goals. By seeing what I want and feeling excited about it, my subconscious goes to work helping me to create my dream life. My vision board always works for me and I love finding old vision boards and marvelling at the fact that I achieved almost everything that was on there.

A few years ago my husband Anthony and I decided that we wanted to go to Egypt. So we cut out some pictures of Egypt - the pyramids and camels - and stuck them on our vision board. We had no idea how we were going to make it happen at that stage or how we would fit it into our schedule. So we just got on with our lives and kept focused on our business and family goals for the year. A few weeks later we received an invitation to attend a Billionaire Bootcamp in Egypt run by personal development guru Christopher Howard. It was an opportunity to be mentored by Chris, do some charity work in Egypt and have an adventure at the same time. It was perfect and off we went four months later!

Enjoy this process: start collecting pictures and images from magazines. Find pictures of things you have decided you want in your life and then have some fun and create your very own vision board. It's something you can also do with the kids, your partner, friends, or parents.

Make sure you hang your vision board in a place you will see it regularly and be sure to update it at least once a year. This keeps the images fresh in your mind.

In addition to a vision board, some of my friends have made video montages of the images on their vision boards. Using a digital program (for example www.mindmovies.com) – and there are a number available online – you can create a video using digital images of the experiences you want in your life and add your favourite song to really feel the emotion when you watch it.

Chapter 2: It's Time To Dream

Take time out to visualise

Another great visualisation practice is actually taking time out to close your eyes and imagine your dreams as if they were happening. See yourself driving your dream car or holding your healthy baby, see yourself and your family on your holiday to Disneyland or imagine that you're being handed a cheque for $1 million.

Whatever your dreams are, visualise them actually happening. I like to do this when I first wake up in the morning, and whenever I am just sitting in a quiet place with a few minutes to spare, like when I am waiting at the school to pick the boys up or when I'm on a flight. Not only does it feel wonderful to see your dreams coming true, it is so relaxing and always puts a smile on my face.

And remember, your subconscious can't separate reality from the dream, so the more you see your dreams the more likely they are to come to fruition.

Be thankful in advance

In Chapter 1 we talked about gratitude and being thankful for the people and experiences in your life right now. We're going to take this a step further and be grateful for what we want to attract into our lives!

I was first introduced to this concept in Rhonda Byrne's book *The Secret*. When we are thankful for what we want to bring into our lives we are releasing a positive vibration into the universe, and this helps us to attract it. Each day when you're writing down what you're grateful for, add a few thank yous in there for the experiences and things you want in your life, making sure to write it in the present tense. If the goal you wrote down earlier was to earn $5000 passive income each month by December 2014, you could write, 'I am so grateful now that I am earning $5000 a month in passive income'. Or if your goal was to own a BMW, you would write, 'I am so grateful now that I am driving my new white BMW'. If your goal is to improve your weight and health, you could write, 'I am so thankful now that I am at my ideal weight and I feel great!'

If you feel skeptical about this idea, set that skepticism aside for a while and give it a try. At the very least you will feel great while you are doing this and for some time after (kind of like feeling better after exercise). At the most, you are taking a significant active step towards really achieving that goal.

What do you say about yourself? What do you say to yourself?

I remember some years ago catching up with a friend of mine named Clare and noticing how much she criticised herself. 'I'm hopeless,' she'd say. 'Trust me to get it wrong, I'm so stupid', and 'I could never run my own business, I'd get everything messed up because I'm so unorganised.' Of course, she was right because she got what she focused on. She knew she needed to change her opinion of herself for her life to start moving in the right direction.

Chapter 2: It's Time To Dream

It is vital that we use positive language about ourselves because the words we speak and think are what our minds are going to believe as fact. If we continue to say that we're silly, or hopeless, that is exactly what we're going to believe about ourselves. And if your belief is that you're stupid and hopeless, do you think you're going to believe that you can earn $1 million this year?

Start to be aware of your thoughts and language and when you notice yourself thinking or saying something negative about yourself, immediately stop and change it to a positive. If you find yourself saying, 'I can't do that', stop and say, 'I can do that', or 'I am happy to give it a go', and instead of saying, 'I can't afford that', ask yourself, '<u>How</u> can I afford that?'

The first step to change a negative internal monologue is awareness. Try to slow down and observe those thoughts: what are you saying to yourself? How do you talk to others about yourself? Or, when you are feeling bad, ask yourself what thoughts have led you to feel that way. One by one, you can start to change your thoughts and your feelings for the better.

Also start the practice of consciously choosing positive affirmations to repeat to yourself as often as possible. For example, 'I am safe and supported', 'I am happy and healthy', 'I approve of myself', ' I am a great businesswoman', 'I am an excellent mother and have great relationships with my children', and 'Money comes to me easily'.

Imagine how much better you'll feel about yourself when you say positive affirmations, rather than negative?

Be positive about other people as well. If you get involved in gossip and negative talk about other people, you're emitting negative energy and can only attract the same level of energy (gossip) back to you. Be mindful too about how you make others feel. One of my favourite sayings is, 'I've learned that people will forget what you said, people will forget what you did, but people will never forget how you made them feel' (Maya Angelou). The more people we help, the richer our lives are.

A great little book to read about affirmations is called *You Can Heal Your Life* by Louise L. Hay. Louise suggests a variety of different affirmations for all different areas of your life including prosperity, relationships, work and health.

By the way, last time I met my friend Clare for coffee she told me how good she was feeling about herself and that her small business was booming!

What is your personal mission statement?

In Chapter 1 we talked about values and how they shape the decisions and choices you make. Family is my highest value and my role as a mother and wife is my most important role right now. To be very clear about this role I decided to write a mission statement, which also extends to other relationships in my life.

Chapter 2: It's Time To Dream

My mission statement is:

> *For my family I will build a healthy, caring and nurturing environment around loving relationships that empower everyone to grow. My family is my greatest treasure.*
>
> *In all relationships I will show honesty, integrity, consideration and compassion. I will help others find their purpose in life. I will nurture hope, see good in all and smile at everyone.*
>
> *At work I will build a fault-free learning environment, which fosters growth and a desire to work with others to discover and fulfil personal and common goals.*
>
> *I will leave everything better than I found it and remember that my mind and body are my true assets.*
>
> *I will use all my potential!*

You might want to find an hour to start thinking about what your mission statement should be. Some people will share this with family and friends and others will keep it as their own personal motivational story. Either way, it helps to have this to keep you on your true path. Indeed it may guide you to working out exactly what your true path is.

Another example of a mission statement is:

> *To live my life in balance with healthy mind and body*
> *To live a life of integrity and honesty*
> *To build trust in family, friends and associates*
> *To be a good father, husband and mentor*
> *To be compassionate and nurture joy and happiness*
> *To build on opportunities and be content with life*
> *To listen first – seek to understand*
> *To develop my full potential and help other achieve theirs*
> *To start the future now.*

> 'Happiness is someone to love, something to do, and something to hope for.'
>
> ~ Chinese Proverb ~

Remember that setting goals, defining your dreams and designing vision boards is an ongoing process. As you achieve goals you are going to want to set new ones but you may also find that YOU change and your desires change as you do more and more personal development. There may be times when you cross goals off your list or adjust your requirements. As long as you are excited and passionate about a goal, it will work for you. If you lose passion or no longer want to work towards something you had previously been excited about, simply set a new goal. The key is to always be working towards something that is important to you.

Chapter 2: It's Time To Dream

Action plan

Write the answers to these questions in your Wealth Creation Journal or in the space provided.

What are you going to achieve in the next 90 days?

_____

_____

_____

_____

_____

How are you going to achieve it?

_____

_____

_____

_____

_____

Who do you need support from in order to make it happen?

___

___

___

___

What affirmations are you going to use daily to support this action?

___

___

___

___

What are you grateful for right now?

___

___

___

___

Chapter 2: It's Time To Dream

List five positive things about yourself:

1. _____

2. _____

3. _____

4. _____

5. _____

Recommended reading

The Seven Spiritual Laws of Success: A Practical Guide to the Fulfilment of Your Dreams, Deepak Chopra

Jack Canfield's Key to Living the Law of Attraction: A Simple Guide to Creating the Life of Your Dreams, Jack Canfield

Awaken the Giant Within, Anthony Robbins

You Can Heal Your Life, Louise L Hay

Creative Visualisation, Shakti Gawain

CHAPTER 3

Creating sources of income

> 'Take responsibility for your finances – or get used to taking orders for the rest of your life. You're either a master of money or a slave to it. Your choice.'
>
> ~ Robert Kiyosaki ~

By now I'm pretty sure you will have written a goal about wanting to increase your cash flow or at least the thought has crossed your mind as you've read the first two chapters. Now it's time to work out exactly how you're going to create that income – and remember; marrying a rich man or a win in the lottery is not a reliable plan!

You may have written one or more moneymaking ideas as you've been reading the book or ideas from years ago are resurfacing. If you're a bit stuck, ask a trusted friend, colleague or family member to brainstorm with you. Ask if they can think of a skill, resource or service you are good at that you could make money from.

As you start to visualise your success and what is possible for you, your intuition may guide you to an amazing idea. So take notice of those thoughts, feelings and 'signs'. Make sure to keep a pen and paper by your bed at night in case a great idea comes to you in your sleep. I always keep a little notepad in my handbag as well, in case an idea comes to mind while I'm out and about.

Chapter 3: Creating sources of income

Your greatest success as far as creating income is concerned, will come when you find a way to earn money from your passion, or when you get passionate about the way you are earning money. Either way, your motivation and energy will come from loving the contribution you are making in the world.

The previous chapters and exercises are designed to help you get closer to finding your passion. Some of you may know exactly what your passion is and how you can make money from it, others might still be wondering how you are going to make one cent! Whichever end of the spectrum you're on, it's okay – everyone is different and will progress at a different pace. Don't compare yourself to others; just stay focused on what you want and how you can get it.

What are your skills?

One of the fastest ways to start earning some extra income is to use the skills you already have. For example, if you're a keen gardener, can you sell the flowers or herbs you grow in your garden? If you sew, can you start a small alterations business by letting your friends and family know?

A friend of mine is a writer and when she decided to go out on her own in business she got started by doing small writing jobs for businesspeople. She wrote website pages, media releases and brochures. She has now worked for herself for more than two years.

Another friend who used to be a hairdresser absolutely loves dogs and wanted to work for herself as a dog groomer. She has started grooming dogs on the weekends and plans on growing her weekend work into a full-time business.

Designer clothes were a passion of another friend, but she couldn't justify the price of the clothes if they were just for her to wear. She built a wardrobe of designer clothes and rents them out for a night so other ladies can wear beautiful dresses for special occasions. She makes money out of her passion.

Let's brainstorm some other ideas:

- Can you draw – where could your drawings be used?
- If you can sing – can you develop marketing jingles?
- Are you a good cook – what niche could you service?
- If you can design a website – where can you advertise your skills for profit?
- Do you have resources to rent e.g. storage space, tools, or the ability to type – where can you advertise them?
- Perhaps you have the gift of the gab and love to sell - what products do you believe in that will give you the biggest return or greatest pleasure?
- What expert knowledge do you have that you could speak about? Could you teach people how to sell?

Chapter 3: Creating sources of income

- If you're a builder or handyman – is there a product people need that you could build, or could you start doing odd jobs for people living in your suburb?

- If you have special knowledge put it on paper and see if you can sell an e-book on Amazon. For example, you might be a scrapbook enthusiast who has a wealth of valuable creative information, or perhaps you're a whiz in the kitchen and have 100 different Pavlova recipes that you could turn into an e-book.

If you've invented something and you see a need for it in the marketplace, ask for advice about how to get it made. Write a list of 100 ways to sell your product and get it out into the market. These ideas may not seem realistic but give your brain the exercise of coming up with as many ideas as possible and then let your subconscious process them overnight for more clarity.

What have you come up with? Write down your skills and some ways you could make money from them.

_____

_____

_____

_____

From babies and Brazilian's to best-selling author

When Fiona Jones had to give up her career as an obstetric sonographer (scanning pregnant women) due to injury, she was at a loss for what to do. Her expertise was sonography and while she was passionate about property and had studied for her full real estate licence while building an investment portfolio, her interest in business was bubbling to the surface. With absolutely no experience in the beauty industry she decided to open a specialty Brazilian waxing salon on the Gold Coast. The business took off from day one and two years later Fiona sold the salon for a phenomenal profit.

With the taste for business, Fiona was on the look out for her next project when she was invited to a three-day course on how to write a best-selling book. Six months away from starting a property development, Fiona thought she would have a go at writing a compilation book in which she interviewed male millionaires from around Australia about how they became successful. With no knowledge of the book industry and not being known in personal development circles, Fiona was facing a challenge but with laser focus, she took one step at a time towards her goal of writing a best selling book in two months – eight weeks later *Mr Millionaire* was born! Three years on and the ninth book in the Millionaire series is in production. When Fiona attended that weekend course she had no idea what would eventuate and now she has a successful business that she runs from home (quite often in her pyjamas!).

Chapter 3: Creating sources of income

While Fiona says there is no balance when you start a business, she says it's absolutely worth it. 'Like all busy mums, I learnt to juggle the business with running a household and now also running a small farm. My days usually start at 5.30am to feed the horses and then it's go, go, go all day. To stay on top of things I make sure I am organised and choose carefully how I spend my time. My family is my priority and then I make sure I exercise at least three times a week, meditate regularly and do daily personal development – I usually do this by listening to CDs in the car or while I'm exercising. If you want to have more you have to become more.'

Fiona's advice: 'I am a huge believer in taking the first step, which takes courage, but once you take that step the doors will start to open; you will find the money, the resources and the people you need to make things happen'.

My businesses of choice

Network marketing and real estate are my businesses of choice for a couple of reasons: there are courses available to teach you the ropes, and you can learn by starting small and fitting it in around a job and family.

Real Estate

We all know people who have made money in real estate. In fact, it is said that most millionaires have made their money from property. I'm also fairly confident that most of us would also know someone who's lost money from property.

There are a few ways to make money from property and it's important to understand the difference between investing for cash flow and investing for capital gains. Very briefly, investing for cash flow means the property provides you with a weekly/monthly amount of cash, rather than you needing to spend any money on the property. Investing for capital gain means that you will hold onto the property long term and potentially make money on the property when the market rises in seven to 10 years time (hopefully). In Australia the property is likely to be negatively geared, meaning that the rental income will not cover the expenses and it will cost you to hold the property.

There are many courses you can study about real estate but my tip here is to make sure the course is specific to the country you want to invest in. I have seen Americans come to Australia for a week or two to teach property investing and visa versa and it just doesn't work. So, unless they teach the exact laws and taxes for the country you are living in – stay away. It's also really worth studying a number of different investment methods and learning from different teachers. Don't just invest with the first company that asks you to because it sounds amazing and you're inspired – do your research and make sure the method is right for you and your stage of life. Do you want money now (cash flow) or are you in a position to hold the property? For example, you might not want to invest for capital gain if you're 75. It's always worthwhile speaking to people who have invested with the company or used their methods to invest – ask if they had

Chapter 3: Creating sources of income

concerns and their current success using that method and whether they would invest with them again.

My husband and I started investing in property in 1993 when we were living in Sydney, Australia. We decided to get into property to have that bricks and mortar investment and an asset that could give us future capital gains and leverage. At that stage our properties were negatively geared. When we moved to the States and I started doing study groups with Robert Kiyosaki, Loral Langemeier and Dolf De Roos we were introduced to the opportunity to invest in cash flow positive real estate in areas that were also increasing in value. So we invested quite heavily and at one stage built our property portfolio to 88 residences. We certainly made mistakes along the way and it definitely wasn't all smooth sailing, but once we cleaned up our systems and processes and started investing wisely by making sure we did very thorough due diligence, we slowly saw our net worth and passive income increase.

A book I recommend to start learning about a variety of property investment methods is *Property Millionaire* by Fiona Jones and Nhan Nguyen.

> 'So many of our dreams at first seem impossible, then they seem improbable, and then, when we summon the will, they soon become inevitable.'
>
> ~ Christopher Reeve ~

Network Marketing

I love network marketing because it is something people can do part-time, outside their working hours or around their family's schedule. It doesn't require HUGE capital to get involved and good companies have training, events and support so that a beginner has a path to follow. The downside is that people can start out with a lot of activity but after a few 'NOs' or a few late nights they lose their drive and forget why they joined in the first place. They don't take into consideration that they need to learn the trade before they will get true success. It's like any trade – you don't become a builder overnight; you have to do your apprenticeship and learn the trade.

I must confess before we go any further that I had tried network marketing twice before becoming successful at it. My introduction to network marketing was while at school when I decided to become a 'make up lady'. I started door knocking in my local area, with a brochure in hand and developed a few regular customers. The problem was that my make up spending habit was greater than my income and within a few months I had to ask Mum to 'bail me out'. I eventually paid mum back. What a great learning experience that was. Then in our early 20s my husband and I joined another network marketing business. I wasn't very good at it, in fact I avoided talking to people, I wasn't passionate about the products and at the time I was more excited about going into the city in a suit and being on the corporate ladder. We lasted about eight months.

Chapter 3: Creating sources of income

The one incredible thing I did learn from that network marketing experience was the importance of personal development. I am so grateful that I was told how advantageous it is to read personal development books and listen to great tapes (there were no CDs then!) because one of the key lessons I have learnt over the past few years in business is that mindset is what will make you money and help you keep it.

Fast forward through my career and the birth of my two children and I found myself going to lectures, hungry for financial knowledge. I met a lady at a course in Phoenix and she told me about an incredible product and network marketing opportunity. Actually she called it a business opportunity but I knew what she meant. The product had such great reviews that I paid my membership simply to learn more. I loved the product and my family got great health results so I started sharing it with friends. One thing led to another and suddenly I was earning a six-figure income from network marketing (remember the passive income goal I set in January 2006). By taking action I suddenly realised that this business I had stumbled upon had given me significant passive income, low cost of entry, training by successful people that had gone before me, a wonderful community, no employees, no need to borrow money to start the business, free holidays, new friends and so much more. What I didn't get were the headaches that come with being a boss or risking my family's finances, or the need to invent a unique product or service.

I have often heard people criticise network marketing; one of the criticisms being that only the people at the top make money. These criticisms come from people who simply don't understand how network marketing works. The direct selling industry is highly regulated – occasionally (like with anything) a bad apple gets through or a good apple turns rotten but on the whole this industry has great merit and is a solid, proven business model. Your success depends on you taking consistent and persistent action with the right activities and not stopping until you reach your goals. You can make more money than those who started years before you just due to your hard work, finding true leaders and choosing the right company; a good company will have no limit on your earning capacity. When you are in a direct selling company you are at the top of your own business and your success depends on you! If you want to be at the TOP of a big business then build yourself a BIG business. The more people you help in your team to reach their goals, the more successful you will be.

The learning opportunities in network marketing are outstanding. In fact, nowhere else can you get personal development, guidance and business training at little or no cost. Good network marketing companies put on large seminars and employ exceptional keynote speakers who inspire, teach and guide you. You will be impressed with who you become if you take advantage of the training offered. I encourage all young people to get involved in network marketing and start learning and taking responsibility. This is as good as a Master of Business Administration (MBA) for learning business lessons but it also gives you the potential to

Chapter 3: Creating sources of income

earn while you learn, unlike a very costly and time consuming MBA course. Network marketing does not require that you have a degree or previous experience in business. But to be successful you must treat your business as though you are going to earn $1 million per year and therefore put a lot of time into becoming an expert at your business. Don't expect to earn huge amounts of money until you have put the time in to learn and practice your skills.

If you have spent your life looking for an opportunity but have not found one nor come up with an idea for a product or service, give network marketing a go... a real go, not just a dip in the water. Research the companies available to you to decide which one is a fit for you and then meet with the leaders near you and decide who you want to work with. A good leader will spend time with you teaching you what they know as long as you show commitment and consistency. There is no such time as 'the perfect time' to get involved; the sooner the better because your positive financial future is waiting.

And speaking of time, once you sign up don't waste your time. Use every spare minute on your new business, because putting in the right effort consistently every day can teach you so much and set you on a steady path to great results in the right network marketing company. Using free time productively is one of the keys to why successful people have more and get more done. Network marketing allows you to use those spare minutes and do so in a smart and effective way. Leverage is an important tool in building your financial future. As you accumulate funds you can leverage this money to make more money. Until then you can leverage your time by building a network marketing team. Small, consistent actions can lead to big results over time.

It's important to realise from the outset that just like any business not everyone will want to join you or buy your product. There may be a subset of the population that needs your product but in the end you don't need hundreds of thousands of people to say 'YES' for you to become highly successful. In a corporate situation you do not get the luxury of building as many people below you as you want. There definitely is a pyramid structure in traditional business. You already know your income relative to the CEO or president of the company you are working for, relative to your boss or your bosses' boss. This is where the true salary ceiling exists. In reality the 'top' of the pyramid in network marketing is available to anyone regardless of education or circumstance. This makes it the great equaliser in business and creating wealth. This is true in my own network marketing team. One of our team members, Shelley Ke, joined three years after me and through her hard work and dedication she has achieved a higher level. She is now one of the highest paid females in MLM in the world. This proves there is no glass ceiling in network marketing – your success is not determined by when you join a company but by how hard you work and how many people you help.

People join network marketing companies for many reasons: to earn additional income, to get rich, to be part of a community of like minded people, to promote a product they are passionate about, to be their own boss, to prevent

Chapter 3: Creating sources of income

missing out on something etc. The reasons people quit network marketing companies are usually because they are not advancing quickly enough, they don't feel they are in the right team or they lose belief (usually in their own ability). Network marketing is not a get rich quick scheme. It is a business with HUGE income potential and should be treated as such. More often than not I can pin point why someone is going to quit and it is usually because they have not treated their business like a real business and they have not taken the actions needed to get it off the ground. People quit before they have really taken the time to learn and practise the skills necessary to be successful.

The best reason for joining a network marketing company is to help people, either because your product fills an important need in the marketplace or by showing people how to build a successful business that sets them financially free. The more people you help, the more successful you will be. The more people in your team who achieve their dreams the stronger your long-term prospects of fulfilling your dreams. The next best reason for joining a network marketing business is to develop your own skills in business, in dealing with people and in personal development.

But there are many other benefits to building a business in multi-level marketing. These include:

1. extra income
2. financial freedom
3. have your own business

4. more spare time
5. personal development
6. making new friends
7. helping people
8. early retirement
9. travel (usually as an incentive from your company)
10. recognitions
11. leaving a legacy
12. health (if you belong to a network marketing company with health products).

Multimillionaire investor, businessman, author and speaker Robert Kiyosaki has written an entire book on network marketing. His book *The Business of the 21st Century* explains how he and Donald Trump evaluated a variety of business models and discovered that network marketing was the one that ticked all of the boxes: low startup costs, no groundwork required (that's already been done), experienced leaders committed to your success, creates passive income, and is suitable for part-time until your cash flow grows so you can transition to full-time. He went on to say that network marketing is not only a great business, but it also provides 'real world business education' and a 'whole new world of friends'.

Chapter 3: Creating sources of income

> 'One reason I have such strong respect for network marketing is that it is a genuine equal-opportunity business. Network marketing casts a very wide net. When you look closely at the more than 60 million people worldwide who are engaged in the business, you'll find people of every color and creed, every age group, and every level of background, experience and skill.'
>
> ~ Robert Kiyosaki ~

Your network is your networth

Someone once told me that if you average the income of the three to four people you spend the most time with you can work out where your income is headed. So the suggestion is that if you spend time with wealthy people, you will be heading in that direction yourself. However, I believe your friends are complete packages with different skills and that you shouldn't choose your friends based on their financial situation. Some might be fantastic parents, others athletes, comedians, exceptional business people, artists, great at Scrabble, good story tellers, psychics, teachers, builders, etc. It is important to have a wide variety of friends and to learn from their amazing skills. Your friends might have ideas about businesses you can create, so I definitely suggest you meet with them and ask for their ideas. The main thing is to TAKE ACTION – one little idea can set you on your path to creating a great income and then reaching your dreams.

Business

While property and network marketing are my businesses of choice, there are many more opportunities for you to consider in business. I have friends who have chosen businesses because of a special skill or passion they have. One friend is a fabulous chef so she holds cooking parties in people's homes teaching them new cooking ideas and then they have a dinner party serving everything they have made. Another friend used to be a yo-yo dieter until she found a diet product that helped her keep the weight off, so she got approvals for the product in Australia and sold it online. And I have a friend who could not find good sun safe swimwear for her daughters so she designed her own and had it made to sell on her own website.

Make sure you do your research before you launch into any business though. Spend some time online researching other businesses in the same niche and how yours would be different. Know everything you need to know about costs and predicted income, as well as your exit strategy.

There are courses small business owners can attend for up-to-date information on running a small business and I recommend that you do some of these courses before getting started in your own business. Knowledge is power, so the more you know the better prepared you will be to run your business and handle any obstacle that comes your way.

If yours is a bricks and mortar business, meaning that you have to rent a shop front or offices, this adds a whole new

Chapter 3: Creating sources of income

level of risk and I can't stress enough that you must be prepared to give your business everything you've got. Don't think your own business will mean more time to relax. As Fiona Jones said on page 79, there really is no balance when you start a business, so just be prepared. I am certainly not discouraging this kind of business, just advising you to do your homework.

> 'Opportunity is missed by most people because it is dressed in overalls and looks like work.'
>
> ~ Thomas A. Edison ~

Selling ice to the Eskimos

You've probably met someone who could 'sell ice to the Eskimos' and wish you had just a morsel of their ability. Most of us hear the words 'selling', or 'sales' and we run a mile because our little voice goes into overdrive telling us that we can't sell.

But I'm here to tell you that you can! Remember when your children were toddlers and you had to negotiate with them ALL the time and find ways to convince your child that she WANTED to do something rather than forcing them to do something. You were selling!

You probably have better sales skills than you realise. The best way to work that out is to read a few quality sales training books and compare your abilities and techniques to those in the book. Either you will see those skills in you or you will learn them as you read. Either way you win!

The great thing about selling is that you don't need to 'sell'. If you're enthusiastic, honest, and confident you will make a sale simply by being yourself. Developing and practicing sales skills is an important skill to work on whether you think of yourself as a salesperson or not. Everyday we are presented with opportunities to sell our 'ideas' or 'plans' to make necessary things happen.

> 'For every sale you miss because you're too enthusiastic, you will miss a hundred because you're not enthusiastic enough.'
>
> ~ Zig Ziglar ~

Do you dream of working from home?

It certainly is the dream of many women (and men) to work for themselves at home. And let's face it, working for someone else rarely provides the flexibility we need to work around our family's needs. As I write this it is the last week of school and there are lots of fun events at the school that my kids love us to be part of and we're able to participate in all of them. Only mums and dads who own their own businesses or don't work get to regularly share these events with their kids. The others either feel guilty for not being at the kids' events or feel guilty asking work for (more) time off.

Chapter 3: Creating sources of income

Working at home definitely has its advantages and everyone I know who is in this position absolutely loves the flexibility and choice it gives them. And just as important is their feeling of achievement, working and succeeding at something they choose to do and love.

But before you take this exciting step into working from home, make sure you have weighed up the pros and cons. I have listed some below, but do your own research as well – talk to friends and family who work from home and listen to their experiences.

I work from my home on the Gold Coast and absolutely love it, particularly the flexibility it gives me having two active children. If I am not travelling I can be at all of their school events and participate in the school community.

Benefits of working from home:
- set your own work hours
- easy to pick the kids up from school or look after them if they are sick
- work in your pjs!
- miss the peak hour traffic – no travel time
- no office gossip and no boss to tell you what to do, how or when to do it!
- no large rent commitment for separate office or shop space.

Downside of working from home:

- no social interaction – can feel isolating
- no training department to increase your skills and knowledge
- discipline is a must because it can be easy to get distracted at home
- can be difficult to shut off when you walk past your office at night or on weekends.

Can you think of any other pros and cons of working from home?

_____

_____

_____

_____

I have secure employment, and I'm not sure business is for me

If this thought or something similar has been running through your head, we need to work out why.

Chapter 3: Creating sources of income

Starting your own business is a big step, and we all have financial commitments to meet, so I understand if the thought of starting your own business makes you feel some fear. That's natural, particularly if you don't have a partner to back you up. But would you rather experience a little fear as you take a life changing step, or would your prefer to keep doing what you're doing, and earning what you're earning to stay in your comfort zone?

The great thing about going into business is that there are many ways to do it and you don't initially have to jump in feet first.

Let's take my friend's example of wanting to leave her government job and work for herself. While still working full-time for the government she started taking on some private clients after hours and on weekends. Once she had several clients on her books, she asked her boss if she could work part-time and they agreed as they really didn't want to lose her. Six months later she left her job and became self-employed. At the same time, she decided to move out of her inner city apartment, and move in with family for six months to ease any financial worries while she kept building her business. She feels in control of her life and loves the flexibility of working for herself.

This is a great way to ease yourself into business (and test whether you're suited to business) while still earning an income.

Some people just aren't suited to business though and are very well suited to employment. Perhaps this is you? There is absolutely nothing wrong with this except that you are limited in the amount of money you can earn and must work to someone else's rules. If this is the case for you, then attend real estate investing seminars and see if that might be a way for you to set yourself up for retirement.

Business is really the only way to go if you want financial freedom. I love this quote from Robert Kiyosaki:

> 'If you want a solid future, you need to create it. You can take charge of your future only when you take control of your income source. You need your own business.'
>
> ~ Robert Kiyosaki ~

Another reason to take control of your financial future

Approximately 40 per cent of marriages in Australia and New Zealand and slightly more in the US end in divorce. Additionally, it is possible that our partners could have a health situation that stops them working or takes their lives prematurely. We also know that it can be extremely difficult for families to exist on one income. For these reasons we need to take control of our own financial futures. We

Chapter 3: Creating sources of income

cannot guarantee that an old aged pension will be available in Australia in the near future but we can safely guess that the pension will not cover ALL of our financial needs when we get older. By taking action now, we can ensure we have income in future years and make the outlook brighter. Even if you start to earn an extra $200 a week now, this is setting you up for learning how to make more and more money in the future. Start small if you have to but dream big so you are motivated to take action everyday.

You may not be able to think of a service or product right now but just by opening yourself to the possibility, something could well show up. In the meantime, join some networking groups or start doing courses that get your mind active in this area. Some of the courses could be on-line or pre-recorded so you can fit them into your current schedule. The most important thing to do is to simply start taking action NOW.

Many people complain of a lack of time when really it is a lack of direction. Remember to go back to the previous chapter and get excited about your goals so that it is easier to take action. Baby steps taken EVERY day can add up to AMAZING results over a period of time. And you don't have to be perfect – just keep improving!

A final word on choosing your business

It's going to get exciting when you're brainstorming business ideas and you might just want to quit your job tomorrow and jump on in. I strongly encourage you to do your homework before you jump ship, without of course developing paralysis by analysis! By this I mean that you do so much research that you freeze with fear.

What I would suggest you do is write down what you want from your business to make sure it suits your lifestyle. This might seem basic and obvious but sometimes when we get caught up in the enthusiasm and excitement of working for ourselves, we can forget what we really want.

For example, if you're trying to have a baby it might not be the best time to start a business that requires a shop front. Network marketing might be a better option so you can stay at home once your baby is born. Similarly, a shop front might not be the most suitable choice if you have young children at school and you don't have family living nearby to help with the school pick up and after school activities etc.

Write a list of what you do and don't want from your business. For example:

Do want
- to work from home
- passive income
- online business
- flexibility with work hours
- to outsource to workers.

Don't want
- shop front
- staff
- warehouse
- Monday to Friday, 9am – 5pm work hours.

Chapter 3: Creating sources of income

What do YOU want?

Do want:

_____

_____

_____

Don't want:

_____

_____

_____

This is a very important exercise because you need to be very clear about whether your business idea will also suit your lifestyle. You don't want to focus on what you don't want because you get what you focus on. But you do need to be very aware of what you want to avoid when planning your financial future.

> 'You can have everything, just not all at the same time.'
>
> ~ Oprah Winfrey ~

Action plan

What is the first step you are going to take on your business journey?

_____

_____

_____

_____

What kind of business do you want to get into?

_____

_____

_____

_____

What business books will you read and what courses can you do to learn more about business?

_____

_____

_____

_____

Chapter 3: Creating sources of income

By what date do you want to be working in your business?

_____

_____

_____

_____

How much do you want to earn in your first year of business?

_____

_____

_____

_____

Recommended reading

The Business of the 21st Century, Robert Kiyosaki

Your First Year in Network Marketing, Mark Yanell

Rich Dad Poor Dad, Robert Kiyosaki

Why We Want You to be Rich, Donald Trump and Robert Kiyosaki

Rich Woman, Kim Kiyosaki

Put More Cash in your Pocket: Turn What you Know into Dough, Loral Langemeier

The 4-Hour Workweek, Timothy Ferriss

Instant Wealth Wake Up Rich! Discover The Secret of the New Entrepreneurial Mind, Christopher Howard

Property Millionaire, Fiona Jones and Nhan Nguyen

Lean In, Sheryl Sandberg

CHAPTER 4

Happy Families – Fulfilling Relationships

> 'Happiness is not a station you arrive at,
> but a manner of traveling.'
>
> ~ Margaret Lee Runbeck ~

Have you ever thought to yourself, 'I'll be happy once I get the promotion', 'When we finish building our dream home I will be happy' or 'Once I am married I will be happy'?

Be honest and let's get this in writing. If you've ever had thoughts like this please write them here or in your Wealth Creation Journal.

_____

_____

_____

_____

_____

_____

_____

Chapter 4: Happy Families – Fulfiling Relationships

Now I want you to think seriously about why you would wait until then to be happy. What if the things you're waiting for never arrive? What if you change direction and plan something else for your future instead? Or what if you get to your destination and it isn't as you imagined? Successful people will tell you that you need to enjoy the journey. The ups and downs are all part of the process and every hurdle teaches you the skills you need to reach your goals. Embrace the journey and live in the moment to get the most happiness out of every day.

Some of the happiest people I have met are people from third world countries who barely have any material possessions to their name and live the simplest of lives. This is not at all to say we shouldn't strive for wealth and to have the things we want, but your happiness shouldn't <u>depend</u> on them.

Happiness is not about material possessions or our job title, and it's not something we just suddenly stumble upon. It's something we must work on and create. We can all experience happiness when we watch our children playing, but the happiness I am talking about is one that is present all of the time; it's a feeling of contentment.

The good news is that you can be happy – because being happy starts with YOU!

Let's take a look at some of the reasons that could be contributing to your level of happiness. As women we're often more responsible for running the household and keeping everything ticking along nicely. As a result, we're usually the last ones to have our needs fulfilled; in fact our needs can take a back seat altogether. After a while this can become exhausting and frustrating to say the least.

Feeling that they have to be perfect and invincible is also a trait of many mothers. Our personal expectations are so high; we want to do everything just right and on time. I don't know about you but I don't know anyone who is perfect - no one. Even those people who appear to have the perfect life may be experiencing difficulties in their finances, marriage or health – we just don't know what is happening in people's lives and should never assume. The point here is that comparing yourself to others isn't helpful. Live your life and aspire to your dreams, not those of others (or what you think others have).

We need to accept that 'life happens' to all of us. Things change and challenges arise; family dynamics change as the kids grow and mature. Talk to your trusted friends and share the load; ask them what works for them and hopefully you can have a few laughs about the challenges and family dynamics as the kids grow up!

All of these life challenges can add up to you feeling unhappy or overwhelmed, so you need to make sure you set aside time to nurture yourself emotionally, physically and spiritually. By taking time out for yourself and doing things that you enjoy and that make you feel good will enable you to better cope with the busyness of life and everything it throws at you. It's also much easier to teach your children a sense of self-worth when you feel worthy yourself. So please schedule time in your diary for YOU.

Chapter 4: Happy Families – Fulfiling Relationships

A concerning fact is that the World Health Organisation has identified depression as the largest medical burden ahead of heart disease, cancer, diabetes and tuberculosis by 2030. We all know people who are depressed or very unhappy. Why, if we live in such a prosperous and safe country, are people so unhappy? I personally think it relates back to comparing ourselves to others and where we have been trained to look for happiness. Do you believe the more you have or the more you achieve, the happier you will be? This focus on life achievements or meeting goals is important for your growth and productivity but we need to learn inner peace and happiness that does not depend on external circumstances. Inner harmony that is independent of your financial, career or health experiences is most important to your personal happiness. The goal is to bring happiness to all your life experiences rather than looking at life experiences to provide your happiness.

> 'True beauty and joy in life doesn't depend on how happy you are but on how many people are happy because of you'
>
> ~ Author unknown ~

Strategies to help you cope with a busy life

Work/life balance – is it possible to achieve?

Life is busy; I think we'd all agree on that without too much convincing. Sometimes I feel that there is so much to do that I can't possibly get it all done. It can all feel very overwhelming and out of control at times and this certainly doesn't seem conducive to happiness. So I have accepted that work-life balance doesn't exist and introduced strategies to better manage my time and gain control – and it feels great! You might like to introduce some of them into your life to gain control and start smiling again. I have a saying I tell myself when I get overwhelmed with everything I need to do. I say, 'The important things always get done'. It reminds me that everything is fine and I am doing my best and I am right on track. And history has proven this to be correct because I always make it to the plane and submit my taxes on time.

Focus on the task at hand

Over the years I have learnt to manage my commitments better by compartmentalising my time. For example, between 9am and 4pm I am completely focused on my business and then come 4pm when my boys get home from school I switch off from work and focus solely on having family time. If I have a meeting in the evening, I give the kids plenty of warning and make sure we have used our time well. The kids understand that work time is important for all of us because it pays the bills. They also see us enjoying our work and helping others. When I exercise I put 100 per cent effort into that, knowing that it's so beneficial to all aspects of my life. If my personal trainer asks me to do something hard then I tell myself, 'I can do anything for one minute'. Then all of those short exercises add up to a productive hour of exercise that I feel great about afterwards.

Chapter 4: Happy Families – Fulfiling Relationships

Another great time management strategy I use is time chunking. I'm sure you can relate to a scenario somewhat like this: you're at your desk trying to write an important report that is due today, an email pops up and you get side-tracked replying, the phone rings and the caller needs you to check a document that's in your filing cabinet, you suddenly remember your phone bill was due yesterday and you're expected in a meeting in 10 minutes. By the time you get back to the report it's more than two hours later and you've forgotten where you were up to. We get so easily distracted from the task at hand that it often takes us twice or three-times as long to complete anything. This is where time chunking comes in.

I allocate a certain amount of time to my important tasks and during that time reduce potential distractions by turning off my emails and asking my assistant to answer my calls. Once the task is done I will then move onto the next task and return any calls and emails once the most important jobs are done. It sounds rigid but it works and it works well. Of course you need to be flexible but I try and stick to this for the main part as my work output definitely increases when I chunk my time.

Outsource and ask for help

Another important lesson we must learn is that it's okay to ask for help and to pay others to do the jobs you either don't enjoy or that aren't your forte. I outsource my housework and bookkeeping, and also pay a student to drive the kids to and from school and make their lunches. This gives me quite a few additional hours each week to do the things I cannot outsource in my business or my life.

Are there any areas of your life you could outsource? Remember, you don't have to do everything; it's okay to lighten your load and ask for help. You may want to write a goal for a time in the future when you could pay for chores to be done for you, such as your house cleaning, gardening, bookkeeping etc.

_____

_____

_____

_____

Eat that Frog

You might have heard of this fabulous book written by personal development leader Brian Tracy. It reveals the secrets to effective time management including doing the tasks you don't want to do – the tasks you are procrastinating about – first. The theory is that if the first thing you had to do each morning was to eat a frog, you can be fairly certain that nothing else you do that day will be that bad! For example, if you have to make a phone call that you are dreading, this is exactly the first task you should do in the morning. Imagine how much better you'll feel once the call is out of the way? Your mind is then free to concentrate on other tasks.

Procrastination is all about avoiding something that you're really not interested in doing, so I suggest taking notice of the type of work you procrastinate about and look to outsource

Chapter 4: Happy Families – Fulfiling Relationships

those tasks. If I have a task that I really MUST do myself but I really don't like doing it, I think about how great I will feel when it is done. I know from experience that I procrastinate on getting my tax information to my accountant because paperwork is not my favorite chore. However I also know from experience that I feel elated when I get the job done. So I no longer procrastinate about getting it done because I focus on how great I am going to feel if I put the effort in NOW.

> 'Laziness may appear attractive, but work gives satisfaction.'
>
> ~ Anne Frank ~

It's okay to say no

Saying no is often very difficult, particularly for women. We like to please everyone and this often means our own requirements go to the bottom of the list. The ability to say no, and put your own needs first, or even just higher priorities first, is very important. What really helps with saying no, or making the decision to say yes or no, is to go back to your goals and mission statement to check whether what you're being asked to do will help you to achieve your goals or fulfill your mission statement. For example, if you're asked to sit on a fundraising committee for the kids' soccer club, you would have to work out whether giving your time to the charity would benefit both you (meeting new people, time out etc) and the club. If you have too much on already it's likely that you're not going to give 100 per cent focus to the role. It doesn't mean that you don't want to help; it's just that this may not be the best way for you to contribute at this point in time. Weigh things up and if it doesn't work for you right now, decline the offer with gratitude.

It really is okay to say no.

<u>Learn to let go</u>

There is a lovely book I recommend everyone reads called, *Don't sweat the small stuff* by Richard Carlson. Chapter six is titled, 'Remind yourself that when you die, your "in-basket" won't be empty'. He talks about so many of us living as though we have to finish everything on our 'to do' list before we have fun, or spend time with the family. For a lot of us, our 'to do' lists become an obsession. What Richard reminds us is that your in-box, or in-basket, is <u>meant</u> to have things in it: 'In fact, it can be argued that a full "in-basket" is essential for success. It means your time is in demand!' He says we need to let go of emptying it and accept that there are always going to be things to do and if we don't let go and have some down time, your wellbeing and relationships suffer.

I have learnt to always complete the really important tasks and let go of what I can't get done. It will still be there tomorrow!

<u>Keep phone calls short and productive</u>

I am on the phone a lot in my business. In fact, it's possibly my most important business tool. I make a point of not wasting my time or the time of the person on the other end

Chapter 4: Happy Families – Fulfiling Relationships

of the phone. So before you go on a business call, write down what you need to discuss and get straight to it once you're online. It's not about being rude; it's about being respectful of everyone's time and working effectively.

Don't get caught up in drama

I have a friend whose life was always full of drama. Something unexpected or outrageous would happen to her almost every week and I always heard about it.

Often things weren't quite as dramatic as she would make them out to be but she seemed to enjoy sharing her experiences with lots of energy and enthusiasm!

A few years later she said to me, 'I used to attract so much drama into my life but I have realised that it was because I wasn't very happy and that I was unfulfilled. Now that I have goals to work towards and greater self-esteem, I don't' seem to have the drama, and I am certainly not interested in getting involved in anyone else's drama.'

She was absolutely right! We do attract drama into our lives (often to seek attention) if that's what we are looking for, and make matters worse by telling everyone about it.

Like my friend, finding more meaning in your life and taking time out to look after yourself (you deserve it and this will help to improve self-esteem) and relaxing more, are ways to cut down the drama. Drama uses energy that you could definitely put to better use in other areas of your life.

> 'Being happy doesn't mean everything is perfect.
> It means you have decided to look beyond the
> imperfections.'
>
> ~ Author unknown ~

Relationships play a huge part in our happiness

How would you rate your relationships? Are there any personal relationships that need some extra attention right now, or are you communicating well with loved ones and enjoying their company?

Your relationship with your partners, children, parents, siblings, close family and friends play a significant role in your happiness. Any issues or concerns can affect so many areas of your life, including your health.

You may find that any frustrations will ease once you implement some of the strategies we discussed earlier to bring a little more 'balance' into your life because, if you're stressed, it's only natural that this will take its toll on your relationships.

My other advice is to focus on the things you love about these important people in your life. When you focus on the things that annoy you – perhaps they leave their clothes on the floor, or don't help with chores or always want the last word– you will only exacerbate the issue. Think about the great

Chapter 4: Happy Families – Fulfiling Relationships

qualities in this person and don't get caught up worrying about the little things that really don't matter.

When it comes to your children, remember that they are just that, children. They live in the moment and are great reminders to us all about what really matters in life. Pay attention to the lessons they can teach you.

If there are serious problems in your relationship with your partner, or in other relationships then it might be worth speaking with a professional.

My family is my number one priority so I make sure that they come first and that I dedicate quality time to spend with them and really be present (not thinking about work or the washing). Make sure you are spending quality time with your kids and your partner and really focus on them during that time. Do fun things together and schedule date nights with your partner so that you get time to have meaningful conversations.

If you're a single lady waiting for happiness when you meet your ideal partner, my advice is to start being happy now. When you're feeling better about yourself and your life, you're far more likely to attract the right kind of partner into your life.

Make your relationships a priority in your life.

In her book *Happy for No Reason*, Marci Shimoff says that until we learn to be happy for no reason, your 'happiness is affected by the energy of the people around you'. If you spend time with positive supportive people you're going to feel happy. If however you spend time with angry, grumpy, depressed people, you're not likely to feel very happy are you? So it really is important to carefully select who you spend time with and at the same time, learn to be happy for no reason.

Don't judge others

I have come to realise that when you judge others, you're really just trying to make yourself feel better. Judging and criticising others doesn't benefit anyone.

Everyone is different and will make different choices to you; you might not like the clothes they choose, or agree with their choice of boyfriend, or house colour etcetera, but does it <u>really</u> matter?

Pay attention when you start to judge or criticise others (and yourself) and stop yourself. You don't have to agree with their choice of outfit or their behaviour, but you also don't have to make them wrong for it (unless of course they are breaking the law or causing harm to themselves or others).

When you are less critical of others (and yourself) and more focused on becoming a better person, you will notice a difference in yourself and what you attract into your life.

Don't try to change others by pointing out their 'weakness'. If you want to influence others it's best to simply lead by example.

Chapter 4: Happy Families – Fulfiling Relationships

> 'When we judge or criticise another person, it says nothing about that person; it merely says something about our own need to be critical.'
>
> ~ Richard Carlson ~

Achieve more PBs

When we're less focused on the 'weaknesses' of others and more focused on becoming the best person we can be, life is much more fun! I am very focused on always improving myself as a person, wife, mother, friend, businessperson, mentor, horse rider etc. To do this I try to always strive towards achieving PBs (personal bests). For example, if I contacted 30 potential clients last week, this week I will aim for 40. If I jumped 40cm during my horse-riding lesson last week, this week I would aim for 50cm. Achieving PBs, just like professional athletes, feels great and when you feel great you're getting closer to being consistently happy!

Keep doing the things that make you feel good!

Get rid of your guilt

One thing that doesn't make anyone feel good is guilt. We all feel guilty at times over something we said or did, or perhaps something we didn't do. Holding onto guilt is detrimental to your own wellbeing so you really need to deal with it and move on.

Sometimes a simple conversation with a trusted friend can help to ease the feelings of guilt. I know a lot of mothers feel guilty because they feel they should spend more quality time with their children, rather than working. If you discuss this with your friends who also have children, I'm sure you'll be able to come up with a perfect solution or realise that you are an amazing mother just as you are right now.

Other times it may be that you need to work through your guilt with a professional. Either way, it's really important to free yourself of any guilt as it stifles you from feeling free and happy.

Stop thinking – start doing

Just like water stagnates when it stops moving, so to do human beings. Have you ever noticed that the less you do the more tired and uninspired you feel? I've often heard people who are overweight say they're too tired to exercise. So they stay on the lounge and continue to feel sluggish. Remember what happens to water when it doesn't move.

And this doesn't just relate to exercise. You need to stop just wishing for your dream life and start <u>working</u> towards achieving it.

Stop thinking about what you want to do and start doing it! Taking action and getting results is so satisfying that you can't help but feel wonderful!

Chapter 4: Happy Families – Fulfiling Relationships

Cheerleaders

I have asked my family to be my biggest cheerleaders and I am theirs. It is too easy to look at things your loved ones do and try to 'help' them by pointing out their actions and 'telling' them how to improve without adding compliments and telling them how much you admire them. It is important to praise all your family members when they try something or achieve something or continue to do things correctly.

I am skiing in the US while writing this chapter and a great example comes to mind. In previous years I told my husband that I didn't want 'ski tips' from him, as they seemed to come at times I wasn't feeling confident anyway. He was upset that I would rather pay an instructor than listen to him as he is a great skier and knows how to teach. But this year something changed. Both he and his brother (who is also an awesome skier) started to praise what I was doing. They described exactly what I was doing right and I found myself concentrating on what they were describing and I therefore kept improving. They were my biggest cheerleaders so on occasions I was content to let them be my coaches as well. It felt so good to have people cheering my successes.

Sit down with your family and talk about being there for each other, cheering each other on in all areas of their life. There are enough people out there criticising or giving us advice so keep your family tight and watch each other for all the good things you are all doing and you will build a stronger family unit where people feel safe and are happy to take risks.

> 'Do all things with love.'
>
> ~ Og Mandino ~

Action plan

What strategies are you going to introduce to gain some control in your life? For example, outsourcing, saying no, time chunking.

_____

_____

_____

_____

What relationships do you need to work on?

_____

_____

_____

_____

Chapter 4: Happy Families – Fulfiling Relationships

Have you been judgmental of anyone in the past month? If so, write down what you judged them about.

_____

_____

_____

_____

What do you feel guilty about? How can you eliminate this guilt?

_____

_____

_____

_____

What personal bests (PBs) are you aiming for this month?

_____

_____

_____

_____

Recommended reading

Personality Plus: How to Understand Others by Understanding Yourself, Florence Littauer

Men Are from Mars, Women Are from Venus: The Classic Guide to Understanding the Opposite Sex, John Gray

The 7 Habits of Happy Kids, Sean Covey and Stacy Curtis

Happy for No Reason, Marci Shimoff

Children are from Heaven, John Gray

What you think of me is none of my business, Terry Cole-Whittaker

Don't sweat the small stuff…and it's all small stuff, Richard Carlson

CHAPTER 5

Spiritual Abundance

Have a purpose without knowing all the answers

I love that we live in a multicultural society in which everyone has different spiritual beliefs, drivers, ideals and motivations, and that we are free to pursue these in our own way.

Whatever your spiritual beliefs, give yourself time to connect with them. The best way to do this is to have quiet time. Quiet time each day to either plan your intentions, to think about what you are grateful for or to pray can boost your entire system; it improves your immune system, helps you proactively plan your day or sets you up in a great mood that can assist you throughout your daily activities. Start simply, maybe for the two minutes when you're brushing your teeth, a part of your drive or commute to work or before you jump out of bed and start your day. Make this time a gift you give yourself every day and it will become something special that you look forward to. In time you can learn meditation techniques or find a form of movement like Tai Chi or yoga that help you in this process.

Our spiritual self is our essence; it is what makes us alive and human. We cannot ignore that essence if we are to grow to our greatest potential. This is the starting point for every idea we have. A lot of the time we drift through our day or week not feeling connected to anyone or to nature. Consciously being aware of how we exist in nature or connect with others keeps us grounded and feeling like we are part of the grand universe.

Chapter 5: Spiritual Abundance

> 'We are not human beings having a spiritual experience. We are spiritual beings having a human experience.'
>
> ~ Pierre Teilhard de Chardin ~

What makes you feel good?

Doing something that makes you feel good is also a great way to connect with your spiritual beliefs and this is key to getting the most out of life. When you are feeling loving, happy, grateful, appreciative, prosperous and full of abundance, you attract those things into your life and the cycle expands.

Researchers studying happiness have found that the elements people crave like money, social status and possessions do not guarantee a feeling of wellbeing. Instead, finding JOY in the present moment increases satisfaction, improves wellbeing and allows us to live longer and more fulfilling lives. Therefore we need to focus on having the EXPERIENCES that make us feel good and then live in gratitude at having those experiences.

I use music to put me in the right frame of mind for my day. I choose songs that I know will make me feel great. If I told you my list of favorite songs there's a good chance you'd laugh and tell me I have bad/old taste in music but my playlist always puts a smile on my face. When I am in the car I sing really loudly and pretend I am fantastic. It can be really funny when I am stopped at lights singing away and the person in the next car sees me – they usually smile too.

Others choose a walk on the beach or in the park or meditation to start their day (more about this in Chapter 6).

On a family holiday once I took an art class, not because I expected to produce anything good I just did it for fun. I loved it and felt so good for trying something new and as an added bonus I found it completely relaxing. What I also loved about the art class was that it was completely right-brain (creative) and I am generally such a left-brain person (logical, analytical). Last month on our Alaska cruise I did the flash mob dance class and performed for a surprised crowd. This was way outside my comfort zone but a very memorable and fun experience. Don't be afraid to try something new. You might just surprise yourself and tap into your feel good mood.

Are you 'miles away'?

Have you ever been sitting in a meeting and when you're asked a question, you have absolutely no idea what they have been talking about because you were thinking of the conversation you had with your partner last night? Or perhaps your daughter is talking to you and suddenly you realise you haven't listened to a word she's said because you're thinking about what to cook for dinner tonight? Most of us are guilty of this. We're doing one thing but our mind is elsewhere, thinking about what happened yesterday or five years ago, or what we have to do when we get home. We tend to miss out on so much because we aren't paying attention to what is

Chapter 5: Spiritual Abundance

happening around us. And if we ARE noticing things we are judging everything.

Living in the present moment and being aware of what is happening around you is called 'mindfulness'. It doesn't mean that you don't consider or plan your future, because, of course that is essential. It just means that you don't miss out on what is happening around you today. It also means that you're not stuck in the past. Being stuck in the past does not help you achieve current and future goals. Your future is determined by what you do today.

Research suggests that mindfulness can reduce stress, bring more calm and peace to your life, and enable you to think more clearly. It is also said to be beneficial in the way we react to things like mistakes and disappointments. We can't control everything that happens in life, but we can control how we react and what we focus on. I would strongly recommend that you let go of what you can't control and focus on what you can control.

Do you love yourself?

Please be serious about this question because it is so important. All of the work we are doing together won't get you where you want to go if you don't love yourself. Of course I don't mean that you are arrogant and snobby, but that you like who you are, feel worthy and respect yourself – you have healthy self-esteem.

It's funny because when we feel like someone is not doing the right thing by us we are generally quick to get upset about it and want an apology. Yet, many of us do the wrong thing by <u>ourselves</u> and don't think twice about it. We speak negatively to ourselves and internally say things that we would never ever say to anyone else; that is disrespectful to ourselves. Are you doing the right things by yourself? Are you respecting yourself, your decisions, and your abilities? Are you speaking to yourself as you would speak to your best girlfriend? Do you focus on what you <u>can do</u> and what you <u>have achieved</u> rather than on what you feel you can't do or the mistakes you have made in the past? It's time to be kind to yourself!

> It's in the reach of my arms
> The span of my hips,
> The stride of my step,
> The curl of my lips.
> I'm a woman
> Phenomenally.
> Phenomenal woman,
> That's me.
>
> ~ Maya Angelou ~

In Chapter 1 I asked you to write a list of personal accomplishments you are proud of (refer back to page 16). If you haven't had a chance to complete this exercise I encourage you to do it now. I know it will put a smile on your face!

Chapter 5: Spiritual Abundance

Once that is finished, I want you to start making a list of your positive qualities and abilities – what do you like about yourself? You are <u>awesome</u> remember, so your list is going to be long. Your list could include things like:

- I can cook great pasta
- I am a talented … designer, parent, storyteller, writer etc
- I have grown a fabulous herb garden from scratch
- I smile a lot and look for the good in people
- I am intelligent
- I have wonderful relationships
- I can save money
- I have brought up incredible children
- I am a good swimmer
- I can play tennis well
- I am organised
- I am good at my work
- I am good at customer service
- I care about people
- I am optimistic
- I am a good leader
- I show appreciation to the people around me.

Add to this list whenever you think of something you like about yourself. As women, I find that we are too quick to criticise ourselves and never fast enough to praise ourselves. This is totally the wrong way around – we must focus on the things we can do and the things we like about ourselves. You will begin to feel so much better just by changing your focus.

Boost your self-esteem

Goal setting and achieving those goals is great for building self-esteem. Go back and make sure you have set your goals. We talked about goal setting on page 46. Return to the goal section now and make sure those goals are written down, if you haven't already done so. Remember to make them realistic and make sure they are goals YOU want, not what you think you <u>should</u> have.

The way you speak about yourself is also critical to healthy self-esteem. Be aware of the words you use to describe yourself or your behaviours. When you catch yourself speaking negatively about yourself just stop and either don't finish the sentence or rephrase it. For example, if you're invited to do something, instead of immediately saying, 'I could never do that, I'd be hopeless' you could say, 'I've never done that before but I'd love to give it a try'. And when you're pleased with something you do, praise yourself: 'I'm really happy with the way that turned out, I did a great job.'

I was in a beautiful second hand bookshop recently when I came across a great little book called *Sorting Out Self Esteem* by clinical psychologist Grant Brecht. He recommends a simple

Chapter 5: Spiritual Abundance

exercise that will help make you aware of your negative talk. He suggests wearing a rubber band on your wrist and whenever you realise that you're criticising yourself, pull the rubber band. By getting your attention with the flick of the band, you can then stop yourself mid sentence and replace it with something positive and useful. Remember my friend Clare (see page 64)? Once she changed the way she spoke about herself and her situation, many areas of her life really started to improve.

Another way to boost your self-esteem is to start saying 'no'. If you really don't want to do something just say something along the lines of, 'Thank you for the invitation but I won't this time'. You don't need to give a reason or make up an excuse. This is all about taking control of your life, and it is your life so take hold of the wheel. Know too, that it's perfectly okay, and your right to express your own opinion – being assertive is good for you.

Remember to choose wisely who you spend time with and who you have relationships with. If people are negative and put you down, that's not going to help your healthy self-esteem. A friend of mine was in a relationship with a man who often put her down, both in private and in public. He criticised the way she cooked, the way she gardened, the way she painted, how she treated the kids, how she talked to people etc. She got to the point where she was too scared to have a go at anything around the house because she knew she'd be doing it wrong in his opinion. When the relationship ended and she moved out, she said her self-esteem gradually began to rebuild. She said it was like she was getting back to her old self, the person who would give things a go, and have some fun without fear of criticism. Choose wisely who you spend time with and only spend time with positive people who genuinely want the best for you.

And please stop comparing yourself to others. This is your life and if Mrs Jones down the road has a nicer car than you does it really matter? Live your own life and of course strive for the things you'd like, but not because you want to keep up with the Jones'.

Just like anything we learn in life it takes time and practise to learn to love and accept ourselves just the way we are. I can't stress enough just how important this is though - please be kind to yourself and focus on the positives.

How do you see yourself?

If you want to be a successful businesswoman, your self-image – how you think others view you - must correspond. If you think that people perceive you as a low achiever who hasn't really done anything with herself, that's not a solid foundation from which to build an extraordinary life. Your self-image must correspond to someone who achieves the kind of success you are working towards.

Once your self-esteem begins to improve, so too could your self-image. Begin to see yourself as the amazing woman that you are. And remember, we've all had different experiences in life and sometimes you might need some additional support from a professional – we all need this sometimes.

Chapter 5: Spiritual Abundance

Do you have limiting beliefs?

We all have different beliefs and values that we accumulate since birth, which are shaped by our family and associates and the environments we are exposed to. Let's focus on the beliefs you have about <u>yourself</u>. I believe that I am a good person worthy of love and great experiences in life. What do you believe about yourself? Write your beliefs in the space below, or in your Wealth Creation Journal.

_____

_____

_____

_____

_____

_____

_____

Unfortunately sometimes our self-beliefs limit us from doing and being everything we want. They hold us back from living an extraordinary life, and no matter how much action we take, we continue to sabotage our efforts because of these beliefs. These beliefs are known as limiting beliefs. For example, 'I will never have enough money', or 'I am hopeless at following through with my ideas'. If on the other hand you believe good things happen to you, that's a great belief and you should nurture it.

If in your list above you wrote down a belief that is negative, and therefore limiting you, this is the one you need to work on. Recognising the limiting belief is the first, and most important step, because until you realise you have a limiting belief you can't change it.

You could also ask a trusted friend or family member if they have heard you say anything negative about yourself. If you have and you've said it often this may also be a limiting belief. Sometimes they are subconscious, so asking a trusted friend is a great way to help uncover them.

Once you have uncovered your limiting beliefs, it's time to get to work on changing them to a more helpful belief. There are various methods used to change limiting beliefs but using these three steps is a good place to start.

Step 1: Recognise the limiting belief. For example: 'I am not good enough.'

Step 2: Be aware of when that limiting belief is surfacing and notice how it makes you feel. For example, if you catch yourself thinking, 'I am not good enough to get that job, or be invited to that event' etc, take notice of how it makes you feel. It can't feel good to be criticising yourself that way.

Step 3: Change the focus and back it up with evidence. As soon as you notice the limiting thought, change the focus

Chapter 5: Spiritual Abundance

and say something like, 'Of course I can get the job. I won the job in marketing that I applied for two years ago.'

From here on it's a matter of repeating this new habit every time you hear your limiting self-talk. Continue to be aware of your self-talk and then change your focus and support the change with past actions and evidence.

It's likely that you have more than one limiting belief so you will need to work on all of them using this same process. Don't give up on this exercise – remember you want to live an extraordinary life!

> 'All our dreams can come true,
> if we have the courage to pursue them.'
>
> ~ Walt Disney ~

Leave everything better than you found it

If we all did a nice deed for someone or something every day, wouldn't the world be a better place? I try to do at least one thing everyday that will make a difference in someone's life, whether it's giving someone a compliment, or sending someone a card just to say hello.

I read about a successful businessman who quite often goes to the same café down the road from his office. Every now and then as he's paying for his coffee, he pays for two extra coffees and tells the barista to give them to whomever she/

he chooses. I just loved this story – I'm sure he quite often makes someone's day!

Another simple thing to do is to pick up some rubbish when you're out and about. Rather than seeing it and, because you didn't put it there, walking straight past, pick it up and put it in the bin.

Or what about bringing your neighbours wheelie bin inside after it's been emptied, or taking your mum a fresh bunch of flowers when it's not Mother's Day or her birthday.

Ask yourself, 'How can I make a difference in someone's life today?' or, 'Today, how will I show someone that I love them?'

Be a Peacemaker

You only have to watch the news to learn about any number of wars, family feuds or random attacks occurring in the world or in your own community. There seems to be so much anger and hatred in the world, and as a result many people live their lives in fear.

You might think you can't make a difference but you can certainly influence your own decisions and that of those around you by having compassion for yourself and others, and showing love and kindness.

The place to begin is to start working towards peace in your own life. Of course there are going to be days when everything seems to be going wrong and you are just way too busy to feel any kind of peace, but aim for peace most of the

Chapter 5: Spiritual Abundance

time. To do this you need to deal with any anger or blame that you have, resolve old issues and learn to forgive, and this includes forgiving yourself for any mistakes you may have made in life. Holding onto anger and bitterness only ends up hurting you. If you have experienced traumatic events in your life, it's a good idea to seek professional advice and support.

As you find peace and contentment in your own life you will find that more people enjoy being in your company and you will start to influence others to want to live in a more peaceful manner. Holistic success is the ability to make conscious connections with others and feel contentment.

> 'Success is not something you pursue: it is something you attract by the person you become.'
>
> ~ Jim Rohn ~

Are you living with passion and enthusiasm?

I come across many people through my business who are bursting with passion and enthusiasm and it's infectious! I also meet people who are just going through the motions and really not enjoying any part of their life.

When you are doing something that you're passionate about you can never fit enough into a day, you love getting stuck into your work, and work just doesn't feel like work. It makes you feel alive, and remember what happens when you feel great? You attract great things to you.

I am also a big believer in living on purpose. When you know your purpose in life – mine is to leave the world a better place because of my actions – you make decisions based on that. I find it to be a lovely way to live.

Action plan

Start writing a list of things you like about yourself and the things you CAN do.

_____

_____

_____

_____

What activities that make you feel good are you going to do this month?

_____

_____

_____

_____

Chapter 5: Spiritual Abundance

What are your limiting beliefs?

_____

_____

_____

_____

What are your new, useful beliefs?

_____

_____

_____

_____

What nice deed will you do for someone today?

_____

_____

_____

_____

What area of your spiritual life would you like to learn more about or spend more time on?

_____

_____

_____

_____

Chapter 5: Spiritual Abundance

Recommended reading

Real Magic: Creating Miracles in Everyday Life, Wayne W. Dyer

The Power of Awareness, Neville Goddard

Chicken Soup for the Soul, Jack Canfield and Mark Victor Hansen

Sorting out Self-Esteem, Grant Brecht

How to love yourself, Louise L. Hay

CHAPTER 6

Women's Health

> 'To keep the body in good health is a duty ... otherwise we shall not be able to keep our mind strong and clear.'
>
> ~ Buddha ~

Without good health, you can have all the wealth in the world but you won't be able to enjoy it.

The next step on your wealth creation journey is your health. I've decided to keep this chapter relatively short because despite the fact that health is critically important, it really is quite simple to maintain great health. It just seems complicated at times because we are bombarded with the latest research findings that seem to contradict the earlier findings, a myriad of diets and fads confusing labeling and so many products. Combine that with our busy lives and it can become all too hard.

When it comes to health, my key message is to keep it simple.

Move that body

How many times have you decided to start exercising, made a plan, bought all the gear and then quit a few days or weeks later? It's a pretty familiar story because often the plan is unrealistic or perhaps you've chosen an exercise that you really dislike. For example, if you decided to start running five kilometres a day, but you don't like running and you've never been a runner, it's probably going to end in blisters

Chapter 6: Women's Health

and disappointment. Of course it might work for some, but for most people exercise goes through waves of highs and lows and you need to ride those waves by doing something you enjoy and you might just find the lows become fewer and fewer!

On the other hand, there are those who regularly exercise, always have done and always will do. They are committed to exercise because they feel great when they do it and have found the right exercise plan that suits their lifestyle and their personality.

For those in the first category, there are two things missing:

1. The REAL decision to exercise – making a non-negotiable pact with yourself that you will exercise and that nothing will stop you
2. The exercise plan that suits YOU.

Turn to a new page in your Wealth Creation Journal and under the heading, 'My Health', write all the reasons exercise is good for you. Now write the types of exercise you enjoy doing and whether there is someone you could do it with. Look at your diary and work out the best time to exercise and schedule it in. Speak to your partner/family/friend and ask for their support and then make a commitment to yourself and write it down with today's date. It's a good idea to include some reasons why you want to stay committed to your exercise regime and make sure your 'why' is really important to you. Your commitment could look like this: Another example of a mission statement is:

> 16 January 2013
>
> *I, Megan Wolfenden, love feeling great and choose to include regular exercise in my routine and to nourish my body with healthy foods. I am committed to living a healthy life so that I always feel great and have energy to play with my children and fit in all the activities that I choose to do in my day. Being healthy is my insurance for a long, active and fulfilling life.*

It's also a good idea to write this on a piece of paper that you can stick in a highly visible location so you are regularly reminded of your commitment.

Exercise is really important to my husband Anthony and I. We met when we were 19 and he was very fit – swimming and running were his favourite ways to exercise. He had and continues to have a great influence on me and we love to exercise together. We have been rollerblading in San Francisco, mountain biking, snow skiing, scuba diving, water skiing, hiking in Peru, black and white water rafting, abseiling, rock climbing, wind surfing, horse riding, hang gliding, parachuting, ballooning, sailing etc. For all of these activities you need to be functionally fit so we make it a priority to exercise regularly.

Chapter 6: Women's Health

Before we move on to the next topic, I want to be sure you have adjusted your schedule to include exercise at least three times a week. Don't say, 'I'm too busy' because EVERYONE is busy. Find that selfish time to look after yourself even if you have to multitask by making phone calls while you're walking the dog. As Nike says, 'Just Do it!' Do enough strenuous exercise to feel the benefits that include better sleep, improved mood, and increased energy.

If you've chosen an exercise that's indoors, find some time to get some fresh air into your lungs as well. Taking the kids to the beach or walking the dog, or even gardening, is the perfect way to do this. Make this is a natural part of your day, for LIFE!

Are you getting a good night's rest?

When was the last time you had a really good night's sleep? If you regularly get seven to eight hours sleep, that's great because it's just as important as exercise and eating well. If you find you're not sleeping please don't just ignore it and hope it gets better. Do something about it.

If you find your mind is busy, keep a notepad and pen next to your bed and if you can't sleep because you're thinking of things, write them down. Once they're out of your head you might find you can sleep.

Check that your bedroom is conducive to sleep. Make sure you have fresh air circulating through the room and that the room temperature is comfortable. Keep your mobile phone in the office or kitchen, not next to your bed. Turn down the brightness on your alarm clock so the light doesn't bother you and keep any noise in the room low. Make sure your bed is comfortable and keep your bedroom clean and organised. Things like alcohol, caffeine, heavy meals and sugar may affect the way you sleep. Take note of times when you have unsettled sleep and see if it relates to foods you ate the day before.

And of course exercise is beneficial to a good night's sleep.

As a mum, I know that we often let ourselves down in the sleep department. We stay up late to prepare for the next day and get up in the morning before the family. But taking the time to get your necessary sleep now will make you feel better each day and give you more years at the other end of your life. Make sleep a planned, scheduled event that you love to do and wake up feeling fabulous. Work out how much sleep you need and then make sure you get that amount of sleep as many days a week as possible. It really does help with all other areas of your life when you are well rested.

Are you what you eat?

Eating foods that nourish your body is genuinely simple once you are in the HABIT. But I can also understand why it becomes so confusing at times because we are told what to eat, what not to eat, how much to eat, choose low GI, low fat, lite ... and the list goes on. Then there's the 'I'm busy' excuse that pops up all the time in relation to cooking healthy, nutritious meals. Also, we sometimes use sugar or carbohydrates as comfort food when we are stressed or

Chapter 6: Women's Health

tired. Sugar can be addictive and it can take willpower and determination to reduce or give it up.

My advice when it comes to nutrition is to get back to basics. Eat foods that grow naturally like fruits and vegetables and avoid fatty, processed foods. Spend 15 minutes, once a week to plan the weekly meals and snacks and that way you will have all the ingredients you need to stay on track. Make it easy for yourself too by cutting up fruit and vegetables that you can eat on the go. Preparation is key.

I eat a nutrient dense diet to maintain my great health and keep my energy at the levels I need to keep up with my two young boys and my business. I use not only the health products from my company but also those from other quality multi-level marketing (MLM) companies. There are so many good products out there but the key is to do your homework and then try the good ones for yourself and see how you feel when you use them. Natural healing takes time so be patient and do your research and ask your friends for recommendations.

We are passionate about getting the message of good nutrition out to the masses. If someone comes to one of our seminars and then changes to more healthy choices for themselves or their family, then we have had a successful presentation.

Meditation – are you in the zone?

We mentioned meditation in the previous chapter; it is important for our spiritual development and it also has significant health benefits. If the words, 'But I can't stop my mind from racing,' or 'I can't meditate' have crossed your lips, you're not alone. I often hear this from people. The way to slow those thoughts and learn to meditate is practise, practise, practise. When you are ready, I would recommend setting yourself a goal to practise meditation daily for 21 consecutive days and really stick with it. Listening to a guided meditation is the best way to begin. Find a time and place in which you can practise without being interrupted. There are also courses and meditation groups you could join to learn the basics. If you sign up you're more likely to turn up, so this is a great way to learn. You might find that it becomes a habit and that you can't wait to do it everyday. Hopefully you will feel more relaxed, more energised and focused.

Regular meditation is believed to lower stress and blood pressure levels, promote relaxation and improve your immune system.

> 'True silence is the rest of the mind, and is to the spirit what sleep is to the body, nourishment and refreshment.'
>
> ~ William Penn ~

Health and Hormones

As a 40 something female I am intrigued by how complex a woman's mind and body are. So many of us go about our day having excessive thoughts about weight and health, some of us experience anxiety and depression, we worry about

Chapter 6: Women's Health

the people close to us, things that happen everyday, things that happened many years ago and generally over analyse so much of our lives. We honestly don't seem to have a great deal of peace and calm in our lives.

As busy people, we tend to be focused on the negatives rather than the positives, so let's take a minute to focus on the good stuff. As women and mothers we are awesome. Think of all the things you do in a day – you generally run the household, organise the kids, manage the family budget, do the washing and the cleaning, cook the dinner and then you manage to squeeze in your own work and exercise commitments. Wow – that's a lot in a day and you really should recognise yourself for that.

But you know what? I think we could all feel a whole lot better and even more awesome if we really looked after ourselves. If you need to get a bit more focused on your health by exercising more, eating more nutritious foods, and getting more rest, then work out how you are going to do that. I also recommend having a health check with your doctor so that you're aware of your health statistics like your blood pressure, cholesterol and hormone levels. Most of us wouldn't go a few days without checking the status of our bank account yet we go our entire lifetime without knowing the status of our own health. Do yourself and your family a favour and make an appointment with your GP for an overall health check.

I had my hormones checked by a doctor who uses bio-identical hormone treatment and I was shocked at how out of balance my body was. After a few months of treatment I got back to great hormone levels and I feel fantastic; I feel like I could accomplish anything. The little voice on my shoulder has gone quiet and I feel more at peace. I cannot guarantee this will happen for you but I will say that it is worth checking out. I did not realise how out of balance we could get due to the environmental and social pressures we take on. Stress can do crazy things to our bodies and it can be difficult to get back into balance without a little help.

Did you see the movie *Sex in the City 2*? I had just finished reading Suzanne Somers' book *Breakthrough: Eight Steps to Wellbeing* when I saw the movie and one of the main characters, Samantha, credited Somers' book numerous times for helping her to work her way through the 'menopause maze'. I had shared the book with some of my friends so it made for some hysterical moments for us all! That is one movie worth seeing if you need a good laugh.

It really is the best medicine

Speaking of laughter, when did you last have a good belly laugh? I mean the type of laughter that leaves your belly aching? Laughter is an important part of our health and wellbeing. It triggers the release of our feel good chemicals, relaxes the body, and strengthens immunity and eases anxiety.

If you haven't laughed in a while, watch a funny movie, or Google your favourite scene from a comedy series like *Kath & Kim*, or schedule a comedy night at a local comedy club or turn some music on and dance like no one is watching – that always makes me laugh!

Chapter 6: Women's Health

Life isn't meant to be so serious, so make sure laughter is on your 'to do' list.

My top 10 tips to great health

1. don't smoke
2. get plenty of rest
3. eat lots of fruits and vegetables
4. limit your intake of alcohol, sugar and processed foods
5. exercise regularly
6. know your health stats! Have a health check up with your doctor
7. laugh lots
8. maintain fulfilling and satisfying relationships and be useful in your community
9. help others win – be a people builder
10. live in gratitude for the good things in your life – Be Happy!

My final note on great health is to start introducing one change at a time. If you haven't been eating healthy foods or exercising at all, start by reducing the number of glasses of wine you drink a week, for example, or introduce exercise three days a week. A few weeks later you could decrease your sugar intake and add another 30 minutes to your exercise schedule. Gradual change is more likely to be lasting change.

> 'We can make a commitment to promote vegetables and fruits and whole grains on every part of every menu. We can make portion sizes smaller and emphasise quality over quantity. And we can help create a culture - imagine this - where our kids ask for healthy options instead of resisting them.'
>
> ~ Michelle Obama ~

Action plan

What are your current health statistics?

_____

_____

_____

_____

_____

If you don't know them, make an appointment with your GP for a health check.

Chapter 6: Women's Health

What health books are you going to read?

_____

_____

_____

_____

What exercise are you committing to each week?

_____

_____

_____

_____

What activities will you do this week that will make you laugh?

_____

_____

_____

_____

Recommended reading

Ageless: The Naked Truth About Bioidentical Hormones, Suzanne Somers

Five Stages of Health, Dr Ross Walker

Dr Perricone's 7 Secrets to Beauty, Health, and Longevity: The Miracle of Cellular Rejuvenation, Nicholas Perricone M.D.

Simple Changes – Your 100 ways to a Happier, Healthier Life, Philip Day

The Farmacists Desk Reference, Don Tolman

Health & Wellbeing Millionaire, Fiona Jones & Rebecca Griffin with Paul Scicluna

The Secret of Vigor, Dr Shawn Talbott

Superfoods: The food and medicine of the future, David Wolfe

CHAPTER 7

Never Stop Learning

> 'Here is the test to find whether your mission on Earth is finished: if you're alive, it isn't.'
>
> ~ Richard Bach ~

The best way to learn is <u>to do</u>! When you read about ways to improve yourself, you are inspired to take action. It is through continuous action that we start achieving results. Remember there is no such thing as an 'overnight success'. People who achieve a significant milestone have done so through years of continuous effort and continual learning.

Make it a habit to read business and personal development books, listen to audios or attend seminars by accomplished entrepreneurs. Visit your local library and borrow the latest personal development audios. That way you can listen to incredible teachers for free on your iPod and repeat the lessons over and over again. My kids are used to me playing audios in the car and they can even recite certain lessons as though they have met the teachers personally. Bob Proctor and Jim Rohn are two of my favorite teachers because they use stories to teach important business and self-discipline lessons making them easy to remember and apply. I listen to their audios when I am cooking, doing housework, shopping, gardening and going for a walk. Audio means that you can get many hours of education while you are productively getting things done. I make note of the information that resonates with me and then take action on it.

Chapter 7: Never Stop Learning

What was the last personal development book you read, or audio you listened to? Why did you like it?

_____

_____

_____

_____

I have read many of my favourite books several times and repeatedly listened to the audios. Each time I am amazed at how much of the information I seem to be reading or hearing for the first time. In fact, sometimes I feel like I am reading entire chapters for the first time. Has this ever happened to you? The reason for this is that we filter information according to what we are looking for at the time, and according to what else is happening in our lives. You might absorb the information in the chapter about writing a business plan because you are starting a new business, but absorb nothing in the chapter about family trusts, for example. I have read entire books and sat through seminars and 'heard' good advice, but it wasn't until years later that some of that advice actually made sense and had a context. It is for these reasons that I recommend you keep your business and personal development books and CDs on hand (or borrow them again from the library) and refer back to them when you think the content may be more relevant to your current situation. Reread your favourite personal development books periodically – you'll be surprised by how much 'new' information you pick up.

When you find a teacher who inspires you, you will want to go to their seminars or listen to more of their audios. This will re-enforce what you have learnt and keep you on track as you are taking action. Going to their seminars is a great way to meet like-minded people.

I am a big advocate of education but before you sign up to an expensive course or workshop, please do your research on the company or speakers – search online, ask relevant questions and ask for testimonials. Don't just believe their brochures.

Building your financial future is up to you and the only person responsible for keeping you motivated is YOU. If you find you are losing motivation or confidence, go back to your books and audios. Personal development is not something you can do for just one month and expect it to last. Just like exercise, if you want the results, you have to do it regularly and you have to keep doing it.

> 'People often say that motivation doesn't last. Well, neither does bathing - that's why we recommend it daily.'
>
> ~ Zig Ziglar ~

Another great strategy that I find works well during times of low motivation is to look back at my goals and the reasons 'why' I am doing what I am doing. Your goals are so important because they really are your driving force; goals will keep you going when you hit tough times.

Chapter 7: Never Stop Learning

Of course there will be times when you are going to need additional help and support. This is when you need to start looking for mentors and coaches. A mentor is someone who has achieved a level of success you aspire to, has your best interests at heart, has learnt from their mistakes and wants to share their experiences with you. You will need to be honest and respectful of your mentor's time and their willingness to help you. If you are given valuable advice, be grateful for it and show respect by truly taking the advice into consideration. If you commit to doing something, then remain accountable and do it as you said you would.

There are some great financial coaches available. A coach can help you solidify your goals, set action plans and keep you accountable. Paying for a good coach is money well spent on yourself (make it a gift to yourself as this commitment will pay huge rewards if you do as your coach asks of you) as long as you are willing to take action on their advice. I have heard of people who take on a coach and then say it was a waste of time and money, but they also admit to not following through on what the coach recommended.

When you're choosing a financial coach, choose wisely. Remember that if you want to be wealthy, you should only take financial advice from people who have the wealth that you aspire to. Make sure the coach you choose has the training and experience you respect. You also have to 'click' – you want to trust them and feel comfortable to have honest and open conversations.

> 'Education is not the filling of a pail,
> but the lighting of a fire.'
>
> ~ William Butler Yeats~

Affirmations – design your own

As well as reading and listening to the advice of others, what you say to yourself can have a huge impact on your success. We can't expect to be successful if we are always telling ourselves that we are hopeless, useless, or not worthy. What do you tell yourself? It is important to develop your self-esteem and belief in your own ability. Everyone has insecurities and doubts their abilities sometimes, but everyone has something to offer and you must find a way to maintain that value in yourself at all times.

Use affirmations to guide your subconscious. Affirmations are declarations or a practice of positive thinking. Use catchy, positive sentences repeated over and over to yourself to create subconscious awareness. It is a positive thinking technique for change. You can use these sayings to create a powerful and positive attitude to life. Think about what you want to change in yourself and make it a positive affirmation in the present tense and repeat it to yourself many times each day to see results (and be patient with the process). Some examples of effective affirmations are:

Chapter 7: Never Stop Learning

- My body is healthy, fit and full of energy
- I rejoice in the love that I encounter every day
- I have a wonderful partner and we are happy, content and supportive of each other
- Abundance flows freely through me
- I make positive, healthy choices for myself
- I believe in myself and so do others
- I am special, unique, creative and amazing
- My relationships are all loving and harmonious
- Business opportunities are everywhere and are offered to me all the time
- My life is joyful and spontaneous
- Wonderful things flow into my life constantly
- I always get the important things done.

Anthony Robbins says, 'Every day in every way I am getting better and better.' This is another perfect example of a positive affirmation that covers all areas of your life.

Choose a few ideas that are important to you and that will assist you in reaching your goals. Keep copies of your affirmations in obvious places where you will see them often and repeat them out loud when you can. Write these in your Wealth Creation Journal as well.

What affirmations will serve you well right now?

_____

_____

_____

_____

And while we're on the subject of what we say to ourselves, I want to reiterate the importance of being aware of your self-talk. Self-talk is that little voice that pops up from time to time (sometimes too often) to tell you that you can't do something. Do you know the one? Is that voice telling you that you are too busy to do anything else? That you can't cope? That you haven't had a good enough education? That you do not deserve nice things or that you must give completely to your family and achieving anything yourself is to their detriment? REALLY?

Often this voice is based on subconscious conditioning. The way to change your subconscious condition is to train your conscious mind so it knows what is true for you. Make sure you are working on positive, uplifting and forward thinking conscious thoughts so that when your little voice comes out, it is on the same track and moving you in a positive direction.

When you hear your 'little voice', identify what part of you is speaking. Is it coming from fear? Then take a leadership position and tell your little voice that it is not speaking the truth. Tell your self exactly who you are and how you are

Chapter 7: Never Stop Learning

making a positive impact on your life and the 'little voice' needs to move aside. Of course it's best to say it in private, or you might get some strange looks, but you actually need to say it out loud and mean it. Sometimes the little voice is helpful in warning us to be cautious, and these are times we're grateful for it. But when it is negative about you and your abilities, tell it to move aside because you don't need it. You are very capable.

It is time to THINK DIFFERENTLY. Think of all the places you add value, that you are important or where you have great knowledge to share and educate others. It is time to turn off that voice that is not helping you and that is holding you back. Be nice to yourself and treat yourself like you treat your best friend.

Feel the fear and take positive action

As you continue to learn and introduce positive changes into your life you are probably going to come up against some level of fear. This could be fear of change, fear of failure, fear of success, fear of what others think of you, fear of loss etcetera. It takes great courage to really follow your dreams and the person you are today may not be the person you need to be to get to your big goals. We MUST change. Change for the better, that is planned and worked towards, is rewarding and fulfilling. We must overcome any fears that stand in the way of that change. A fabulous book to read about facing your fears, is Susan Jeffers' *Feel the Fear and Do it Anyway*.

Fear can really stop us in our tracks and I know a lot of people who have been held back from pursuing their dreams because they just couldn't face that fear. One of the little strategies I use to help overcome fear is the 'deathbed' exercise. Think forward 50 or so years to when you are lying on your deathbed thinking back over your life. No doubt some regrets will surface. You might regret that you stayed in the job you hated for so long because you were too scared to leave, or that you spent way too many hours at work because you feared not meeting every deadline. You may regret not having travelled more because you were too scared to spend the money … the list goes on. If I have a big decision to make I try to imagine how I will feel about it when I am lying on my deathbed and if I know I will have regrets if I don't do it, I know I can push through any fears and give it a shot.

Don't allow fear to hold you back and keep you average – get over it. If you're worried about what people will say about you, don't be. Some people may tear you down if you have something they don't have. Stay away from those people and surround yourself with your biggest cheerleaders.

> 'For things to change, we must change.'
>
> ~ Author unknown ~

We all make mistakes

As you grow and start to take responsibility for your own wealth, you are probably going to make some mistakes. In fact, every truly wealthy person I have studied has made a number of mistakes in their financial career and other parts

Chapter 7: Never Stop Learning

of their lives. Many exceptionally wealthy people have been bankrupt in their past due to mistakes, but they would not be in the position they are today without having made those mistakes and learnt from them.

Some of the properties we have bought and other investment decisions we have made have been very costly. I remember getting a number of pay cheques and crying that we couldn't even cover the commitments for the week let alone the bills that seemed to keep coming faster than we could pay them. There were times when I didn't know how we were going to turn our situation around. We are still fixing some of our poor property purchases but I look back and am grateful for that education. If we hadn't started taking action we would never have got to where we are today and those mistakes were part of the journey. My goal in relation to my mistakes is to learn from them and not to make those or similar mistakes ever again. I want to get better at pre-empting what CAN go wrong and therefore avoid pitfalls.

Be kind to yourself and recognise that whatever you did in your past has brought you to where you are today. Today you can be grateful for the good things you have and make changes so that the things that don't help you are no longer part of your daily habits and instead, new habits are forming that push you in the direction of your dreams.

Accept as well, that you are going to come up against obstacles as you grow and introduce change into your life. These are part of the journey and moving through these issues makes you stronger and better able to cope with future issues. Think of obstacles as things that need to be overcome. Once you identify an obstacle or challenge, write a list of ways you can overcome them. Take on the challenge - little pieces at a time. Sometimes, as you gain experience you are even able to pre-empt issues and eliminate them in advance.

And if you do make a mistake don't beat yourself up and don't keep recreating the mistake (or past mistakes) in your mind – move on and use the lesson to your advantage. The only way to reverse circumstances is to find the cause and make changes. Words are the foundation of your thoughts. Start there. Positive words create positive circumstances. Think of a potential conflict situation and think how the choice of words dictate the way the situation ends. Find less confronting or accusatory ways of looking at issues. Especially when you are criticising yourself.

When you push yourself outside your comfort zone and feel terrified or confused or hesitant to move forward, this is your time of greatest learning. It is when you are feeling uncomfortable that you are growing the most. Every time you push through and grow, you become better and closer to reaching your goals.

> 'If you haven't had 1, 2 or 3 major failures in your life then you are living a life of mediocrity.'
>
> ~ Randy Gage ~

Chapter 7: Never Stop Learning

Emotional maturity

Let's face it girls, sometimes we make mountains out of molehills and turn a small issue into an excuse or an argument. Yes, we blame it on being tired, hormonal, or just a bad mood. Let me tell you that this is not leading you to a joyous life. We need to be our own best friend and then let others 'be'. Not try to create a bigger situation than it is. Let the small things pass.

As you mature, begin to ask yourself more empowering questions. When a problem arises, ask yourself how you can overcome that problem, what tools you need to work on the problem and how you picture the perfect solution. Asking questions like, 'Why did this happen to me?' doesn't help the situation at all. Ask instead, 'How can I improve this situation?' or 'What can I do to improve this situation?'

Learn to change the moment – you cannot stop unpleasant or bad things happening but you CAN choose to view these things differently. Do you have a half empty or half full attitude to life?

If you have days when you feel sorry for yourself, the best thing to do is help someone else. Give it a go and see how you feel afterwards. A period working for Meals on Wheels or serving food at a shelter puts your problems into perspective and allows you to balance yourself (see Chapter 8).

Only YOU can create the changes you need in your life. Do not focus or blame others. If you are stuck in a process of blaming others for your current or past situation then you may want to see a counsellor who can help you live in the present and release the thoughts that are not serving you well.

Stormy days

My friends, sometimes there are stormy days. We think we are getting our lives on track and suddenly 'life happens'. This is the time when knowing how to be kind to yourself is most important. Sit down in a quiet place with a latte and ask yourself, 'Am I attracting drama into my life or are there things happening around me that I just have to accept and change my perspective on?'

Yesterday I had 'one of those days'. A family friend died after a long battle with cancer. I needed to acknowledge that it hurt to lose such a beautiful person and that my friends were really feeling pain and loss. Later in the day I was thrown off a horse. I accepted that while I won't be riding that particular horse ever again, I do want to continue riding and I must be appropriately cautious. Lastly, my six-year-old son hit his head climbing through a wooden fence and needed a few stitches. Home late after a long stint at the emergency room, running out of petrol on the way home, I allowed myself and my son to have a chocolate indulgence. I had already decided to manage my day with peace and love after the news of my friend's Dad passing. I did not allow circumstances to affect my whole demeanor and bring down people around me.

This has not always been the case in my life. I know of a time when I would have rung every friend and complained

Chapter 7: Never Stop Learning

'poor me'. Dwelt on all the little things and big things that kept happening that day, slept badly and probably continued feeling bad all week.

At different times in our lives we have things happen around us that truly hurt us. These need to be dealt with using many different techniques, love and support. But if you are having lots of BAD DAYS over truly small things when you should be living in the moment and enjoying what you are doing right then and there, then I want you to start training yourself to see the good stuff. Have the innocence of a child and live each day with happiness and gratitude.

> 'The art of living is more like wrestling than dancing.'
>
> ~ Marcus Aurelius ~

Everyone has 24 hours in a day

I've said it, I've heard others say it and I'm confident these words have come out of your mouth too: 'I'm <u>too</u> busy.' And I'm sure you are busy but you know what? No one wants to hear about it and we all have the same amount of time in every day and every week. If you're using time, or lack of time, as the reason you haven't achieved your goals, then think again, because I'm not accepting that excuse and neither should you. All great achievers had the same amount of time in a day as you have.

Time is one of our most important resources and we need to use it wisely. If you find yourself using that as an excuse, it's time to stop! Start choosing more wisely how you view and use your time.

Keep a diary of what you do with your time and look back after a week and consider where you possibly wasted time or didn't use your time to your full advantage. Always be looking at what you do and how you can do it better.

Anyone can succeed!

Think about what success means to you and then see your future self as having achieved that success. Do not measure yourself by anyone else's measure of success, only your own. We all have a success level that we see ourselves capable of. Too often I see people set a low level for themselves and believe that is all they are capable of. Turn your level up – don't get on autopilot and hover below your potential – break through to a new level of success expectation of yourself. With every small success you have and every lesson you learn, use that as a catalyst to push further beyond what you previously thought was possible.

A successful person knows there will be obstacles. These are part of the journey, and moving through these issues will make you stronger and better able to cope with future issues - maybe by preparing for or eliminating them in advance.

Chapter 7: Never Stop Learning

Action plan

What fears are holding you back?

_____

_____

_____

_____

_____

How can you address these fears?

_____

_____

_____

_____

_____

What 'little things' do you stress about?

_____

_____

_____

_____

What images or thoughts can pull you through a stormy day?

_____

_____

_____

_____

Which friends can you rely on to cheer you up when needed?

_____

_____

_____

_____

Chapter 7: Never Stop Learning

How do you cheer up your friends when they need it?

_____

_____

_____

_____

Recommended reading

Outliers, Malcolm Gladwell

The Millionaire Next Door, Thomas Stanley and William Danko

Selling 101, Zig Ziglar

Feel the Fear and Do it Anyway, Susan Jeffers

How to Win Friends and Influence People, Dale Carnegie

The Richest Man in Babylon, George Samuel Clason

CHAPTER 8

The Act of Giving

Only recently have I come to understand the importance of giving back to our community. One of my mentors teaches that, 'When we are blessed we need to become a blessing'. Giving can come in the form of money or asset contribution, time or your knowledge and resources.

My husband and I were recently in Brazil where we witnessed the poverty and immense problems in some of the slums (favelas) in Brazil. We saw children eating out of garbage dumps and living in tiny rooms with no running water and no protection from the elements. They had no power or heat and were living near drug dealers and other criminals. One charity we visited was making a HUGE difference to the lives of thousands of families by providing education, food and a safe place for children to play, with caring adults to talk to as well as training for teenagers and adults to help them get jobs. They also provide safe, warm homes for children without parents and daycare for babies so mothers can find work and therefore provide for their families. The work they are doing in certain cities in Brazil is nothing short of miraculous. They are changing the cycle of poverty, giving hope and love and protecting family units. The people working in this charity are true angels and have given me incredible role models to look up to.

I believe in the power of giving. It is our responsibility to look after the people, animals and environment that cannot look after themselves.

Leave a legacy not only for your children but also for a much wider community.

Chapter 8: The Act of Giving

> 'Act as if what you do makes a difference. It does.'
>
> ~ William James ~

Give a little, gain a lot

The world revolves around volunteers. You may already volunteer at the kids' school, sporting teams, surf life saving, church or other community groups you are involved in. Without volunteers, the events or services could not take place. We must have gratitude for people who volunteer in our communities and around the world and not take them for granted.

I have friends who volunteer to drive elderly people to medical appointments; friends who volunteer at their local school helping students who need extra support with their schoolwork; I know a lady who volunteers to visit an elderly lady in her home and to help her with grocery shopping or take her to lunch once a fortnight; another friend volunteers as the treasurer for a senior citizen's club. We have participated by painting and decorating a women's shelter, cooking at community breakfasts, serving food at food banks, and taking children from an orphanage out for a day of fun and laughter. We have done Clean Up Australia Day, coordinated donations for animal shelters and manned charity stalls. All of these turned out to be great fun and we met wonderful people along the way. These events can also be incredible for team building and helping to foster camaraderie at work.

There are so many rewarding volunteering opportunities to choose from. Often the people volunteering say that they get just as much or more 'reward' from volunteering as the people they are helping. It honestly doesn't have to take much of your time, just an hour or two a week or fortnight, but the difference you could make to someone's life is immeasurable.

Here are some volunteering websites to start researching the various volunteer positions available. There are many other sites:

>www.govolunteer.com.au

>www.volunteer.com.au

>www.worldwidehelpers.org

>www.volunteeringinamerica.gov

>www.i-to-i.com

>www.volunteeringnz.org.nz

When you are in a position to give a little money to charity, start making it a priority. You can start with $20 a week to a cause you are passionate about. Since we were in our 20s we have sponsored children around the world through World Vision and The MORE Project. Through a well-established Australian charity you can donate money so that Australian children can have school shoes, a uniform and books for school. I have friends who donate to a charity in Ethiopia that supports women to gain their life back after being

Chapter 8: The Act of Giving

outcast as a result of a medical condition (known as a fistula) that develops during childbirth. Another friend donates to a charity that helps women survivors of war rebuild their lives through education and small business assistance. There are so many amazing projects and charities you can support that change people's lives.

I recommend having multiple bank accounts that money automatically goes into each pay period for:

1. taxes
2. charity
3. savings (that will later be used for investing).

Pay these accounts first and live off the rest of your earnings. It takes some discipline to do this but you will get used to it quite quickly and then you will prosper in many areas of your life. You can read more about this in the book titled *The Millionaire Maker: Act, Think, and Make Money the Way the Wealthy Do* by Loral Langemeier.

Start looking for a cause to support. A cause that creates emotion and one that makes you feel that your contribution is worthwhile. I find that giving according to your passions to be the best way to choose the charity you will support. For example, if you are passionate about women's rights you would support charities in this area. If your passion is animals, you would focus on charities that provide care to animals. And rather than giving to a lot of different charities that support animals or women's right, be selective and focus on just one or two of those charities. Learn about it and get involved in a way that suits you. You may give money, or you may give time or both.

When you have chosen your charity, you will find that it is much easier to make choices and to say no when you are approached to support other charities whose causes are equally valid.

In your Wealth Creation Journal or in the space below, write down the kind of charity you would like to support. Start researching the various charities that interest you and as you come across a charity you like, make a note of it.

_____

_____

_____

_____

> 'If God has allowed me to earn so much money, it is because He knows I give it all away.'
>
> ~ Edith Piaf ~

Teach your children about service

It is important for us to teach our kids about giving to others and doing service for the community. My husband Anthony and I engage in projects that our two boys can be part of so

Chapter 8: The Act of Giving

they start to understand the importance of giving back and what is truly important in our lives. We also encourage our children at Christmas time to buy a gift from their pocket money for another child their age and donate it to charity.

Some other great ways to introduce your children to giving is to ask them to go through their toys and give away the ones they no longer play with. The same with their clothes – help your children to go through their wardrobe and donate to a charity all of the clothes that no longer fit.

When they are old enough, you might like to encourage them to choose a charity that interests them to volunteer with. If they love animals there might be an opportunity to volunteer at an animal welfare league for example.

Involving children in volunteering and supporting a charity is beneficial for them in a number of ways – by learning to interact with people and making a difference in someone's life, it can boost their self-esteem. It also helps them to appreciate their own lives and the comforts we often take for granted.

Shift your focus

> 'Shifting your focus from getting to giving is not only a nice way to live life and conduct business, but a very profitable way as well.'
>
> ~ Bob Burg and John David Mann ~

Let me say straight up that I do not give to anyone so that I will receive in return. I give because I want to and have no expectations that people would owe me anything or do anything for me in return. It is my pleasure to help other people in some way. I have learnt over the years though that the more I give, the more I receive.

I can certainly think of a time in my life when I wasn't very focused on giving. I wanted to earn more, have more and do more. I wasn't ruthless and nor did I walk over anyone, but I was more focused on my family, and myself rather than on helping others. Some people are so focused on themselves and the outcome they want that they bowl over anyone that looks even remotely like getting in the way. They talk about nothing but themselves and are so desperate to sell you something that it can have the opposite affect. Not only do these people lose friends along the way, they usually end up making enemies! And the money they so desperately wanted doesn't always come their way, or when they get it, they have no one left to share it with.

When I shifted my focus to helping people, everything began to fall into place. And this happened once I found a product that I was passionate about, that was getting great health results for people and giving people the opportunity to build their own business. It was through helping others that I have been able to build a very successful business.

A great book called *The Go Givers* by Bob Burg and John David Mann explains why 'givers' generally experience abundance in their lives, whether that be financial or otherwise. The book suggests that *giving* is the secret to success. This quote

Chapter 8: The Act of Giving

from the main character in the book sums it up perfectly: 'All of the great fortunes in the world have been created by men and women who had a greater passion for what they were giving – their product, service or idea – than for what they were getting. And many of those great fortunes have been squandered by others who had a greater passion for what they were getting than what they were giving.'

The point here is that you can't just focus on what you want to get, you need to be passionate, enthusiastic and genuinely interested in what you are giving and how it can help others, and then good things will follow. Go above and beyond what people expect and then see what happens.

Here's a simple example. A businessman has a budget to meet and the end of the financial year is looming. He is so focused on meeting budget to get commission that his usual high quality of customer care falls by the wayside. Because his focus is so much on crossing the finishing line to get that bonus and not on looking after his existing clients, or on what value he can add to new clients, he starts to lose business.

If he'd kept his budget in mind, but stayed focused on adding value to his clients and genuinely helping them, I can say with certainty that he would have crossed that finishing line with flying colours. By looking after people and keeping their interests at the forefront, you are more likely to keep your clients and be referred to others. Burg and Mann suggest that when you give more in value than you take in payment, your true wealth will be determined.

They also focus on the importance of authenticity if you want to be successful. Being yourself, and not trying to be someone else is the 'most valuable gift you have to offer'. Often in life we feel like we will only succeed if we are more like someone else who is already successful; if I'm more like the CEO of that company, or the director of that business, of if I had the confidence of my friend who is a government executive, then I would be successful. There is room in this world for everyone, and if you <u>be yourself</u> you will find the right people who want to work with you or be part of your life. Trying to be someone else is not only exhausting it's not real. Be yourself and have concern for others.

I recommend reading *The Go Giver*. It's a quick, easy read but the potential impact is huge. This is YOUR opportunity to leave a mark on the world and leave your legacy behind. Leave a legacy by doing something significant that contributes to society. It truly is an honor to serve.

> 'Life's most persistent and urgent question is ...
> "What are you doing for others?"'
>
> ~ Dr. Martin Luther King, Jr ~

Chapter 8: The Act of Giving

Action plan

Which charities would you like to volunteer for?

_____

_____

_____

_____

Which charities would you like to contribute money to? And remember it can start with $20 a week or month.

_____

_____

_____

_____

What do you need to do to organise separate bank accounts for tax, charity and savings?

_____

_____

_____

_____

Recommended reading

The Busy Family's Guide to Volunteering: Doing Good Together, Jenny Friedman

Richest Man in Babylon, George S. Clason

Australia's Money Secrets of the Rich, John Burley

Giving, Bill Clinton

The Go-Giver, Bob Burg and John David Mann

The Millionaire Maker: Act, Think and Make Money the Way the Wealthy Do. Loral Langemeier

Your Mark on the World, Devin Thorpe

CHAPTER 9

Bring It All Together And Make It Happen

It's time for our chat to come to an end. Don't you wish we could stay and talk for hours? I do. But don't worry – we will do this again soon because I can't wait to hear what actions you take as a result of reading this book. Are you feeling happier? More fulfilled? Like you can accomplish anything? That is my hope for you. I want you to feel like you can accomplish anything you put your mind to. It might not happen all at once but at least you can see it all in your future. I want you to 'Be, Do and Have' everything you set your mind to. I want you to feel special, loved and appreciated, and know that you are making a huge difference in this world.

Remember to always be striving to be YOUR best. What do you want to look back on and say you have done well during your lifetime?

Before I sign off for now, I am going to recap some of the most important ideas from the book that you really need to focus on and practice if you want change in your life. And I am confident you do want change if you've been reading this book!

> 'Follow your instinct and have the courage to pursue your dream, despite the obstacles.'
>
> ~ Margaret Olley AC ~

Chapter 9: Bring It All Together And Make It Happen

Make a decision

Before anything changes, you have to know what you want. Take the time to plan your life. Where do you want to live? What experiences do you want to have? Who do you want to have them with? You can't get anywhere if you don't know where you want to go.

Once you've worked out what you want and when you want it, make the genuine decision to start introducing the changes that will make it happen. In my research I have found that the confirmed and solid decision to change must come before ANY significant change occurs. For example, we are ALWAYS making the claim of starting a new diet on Monday/first day of the year/when the kids go back to school etc. But to really make the decision to lose weight and stay on the program there needs to be a very definite decision that you will DO IT and STICK with it (the reasons why are varied but the determination comes when that decision is truly made).

It is the same with any other goals on your list. You must make the solid decision to do it and to WANT to do it. Therefore you may have to start only working towards one or two of your goals until the practice in the right direction becomes a habit. For example, reading books on investing, buying real estate, building businesses or personal development may be foreign to you at first. Make it part of your daily routine, maybe for 10 minutes before bedtime, and within a short time reading at night will become a useful habit. One of the ways I reward myself for reading educational books is to allow myself to read a fiction book after completing three educational books. I look forward to these fiction books and I tend to get through my learning books quicker when I know I have a fun book coming up.

If your goal is to exercise one hour each day but you haven't started any exercise program yet, make the decision to do 10 minutes a day or 40 minutes three times a week until it becomes a habit. Then increase your time or frequency so you eventually get to your goal. The decision to take action is key and you may only be able to start with a few important decisions leading to personal development at one time. That is fine. Just be dedicated to your DECISION!

> 'When you change the way you look at things, the things you look at change.'
>
> ~ Dr Wayne Dyer ~

Take baby steps and you will get there

You might have decided that you need to make a lot of changes in your life or just a few. Whatever the case, you don't need to do everything at once. Take baby steps and introduce change slowly - it will be more lasting that way. You might not always feel like you are making progress but you are! Think of it like planting a seed in the ground. It takes time for the seed to germinate and for the seedling to appear above the ground. We just need to trust the process and be patient, knowing that we have taken appropriate action (planted the seed and watered it regularly).

Chapter 9: Bring It All Together And Make It Happen

We live in a fast-paced society in which we expect everything NOW. When you hear of business successes, so often the media makes claim to 'Overnight Millionaire' or 'Instant Success' but the stories often neglect to tell you of all the learning, trials, errors, bankruptcies and false starts that people have before hitting their 'Rags to Riches' whirlwind. Anything worth achieving is worth working for and takes time and practice.

It is important to set goals and give them a timeline but sometimes we miss that timing. It is OK to reset your timelines on your goals but only reset the timeline if you are genuinely committed to achieving it this time. If you are not 100 per cent committed go back to your goals and choose one that motivates you. Make sure you really are working towards what you want – not what you THINK you should want.

> 'No great thing is created suddenly. There must be time. Give your best and always be kind.'
>
> ~ Epictetus ~

In 2006 we wanted to move countries for a lifestyle change. However the task seemed beyond what I could cope with and I could not see how I could pull it off given we had young children, properties, jobs, investments, household items to move etc. So I broke it down into baby steps;

- save money
- quit my job so I had time to do everything else
- sell the house
- sell the cars
- pack our belongings and send to storage
- ensure my husband's role in our new country was secured and organised
- hire admin support to look after the things we had to leave behind
- find temporary accommodation after we sold the house
- ship household items overseas
- find accommodation in new city
- rent car in new city
- automate bank accounts and bills.

The list went on and on. But as I went through and did each thing and checked it off the list, our goal came to life. Any BIG goal you have needs to be broken into baby steps so you can tackle each one in order. It may take a long time to go through everything on your list to get to your goal, but by eating the elephant one bite at a time you will reach your destination. And that is far better than never getting started and never getting to your true purpose and destination.

Everyday we make simple choices about what we are going to do with our time. A seemingly small decision to watch

Chapter 9: Bring It All Together And Make It Happen

another television show, eat some more cake, sleep in, delay making an important phone call, procrastinating on getting our taxes done or not doing our exercise that day results in a little dropping of our standards. As these decisions accumulate week after week, we can measure a drop in output or delay in getting to our goals. It is important to make good choices every single day. Allow each day to be productive and keep knocking important tasks off your checklist. Take just a few minutes everyday to look towards your future and consider the consequences of your choices. Adjust your choices to ensure success and develop habits that will serve you and move you towards your goals. Success and happiness are a choice. Are you making the right choices for yourself?

> 'Success breeds success and, once we taste the pleasures of succeeding, it becomes too difficult to slip back into our old habits of failure.'
>
> ~ Jim Rohn ~

Be an action-taker

Please don't worry about being perfect. Instead of using your energy on worrying, use it on taking action in the direction you want to head. And if you make a wrong turn along the way, simply readjust and get back on track. You don't need to be perfect but you do need to take significant action and responsibility for your own life.

It works like this:

Decide what you want.
↓
Write it down and commit to it.
↓
Get excited about it – put emotion into your dream.
↓
BELIEVE it can be yours and that you deserve it. See it coming true.
↓
Take significant action regularly.
↓
Re-adjust as you go to stay on track.
↓
Take more action - don't give up!
↓
Watch and enjoy as your actions unfold into successes.
↓
Celebrate!

Chapter 9: Bring It All Together And Make It Happen

> 'Success is steady progression of a worthwhile goal.'
>
> ~ Earl Nightingale ~

Celebrate!

I just love the last step in the process. Please reward yourself when you achieve milestones and reach your goals. Tell yourself that you are proud of what you have achieved so far and share your milestone with someone you trust. For small accomplishments you might treat yourself to dinner, a massage, or a pedicure or for large accomplishments, a special holiday– however you like to indulge!

It really is important to congratulate yourself for taking action.

Take notice of your excuses – they're telling you something

If you find yourself making excuses or getting totally off track just days or weeks after starting down your new path, don't worry. We've all done it. I know I have started something and within days forgotten I had even committed to do it. Or I've set goals, started taking action and then become so busy with 'life' that tasks have fallen off my to do list and before I know it two months have passed and I wonder, 'What happened to my plan to do x, y and z.'

There are many reasons why we don't see things through or steer off our path. It may mean that what you had started wasn't really what you wanted or not something that you're passionate about. Go back to your goals and revise them or make sure they still align with your mission statement, or choose another one, but make sure they fit into the grand picture of what you want your life to look like. Set milestones for the journey to give you results and confidence along the way.

If you feel that the goal is the right one for you but you're still making excuses, perhaps you just need a mentor or coach to help you get started and encourage you on your way. Who could you ask?

If you're worried about what other people might think of you - don't! You cannot control what others think about you, so use your energy on what you <u>can</u> control. Bloom where you are planted.

Sometimes we think we have failed if we find ourselves off track, but this is definitely not the case. You only fail if you quit. Simply re-align your priorities and you'll be back on track before you know it. Life has lots of forks in the road and the action you took in the past helped you get to this new fork in the road. Embrace where you are now and get cracking on achieving new or revised goals. Never, never, never think that because you didn't finish something that you're a failure.

Success is a cycle. You may not be at the peak of productivity and results the whole way through the cycle. Allow the down

Chapter 9: Bring It All Together And Make It Happen

time and keep working towards the goals that you have passion for. Your continued effort will bring new results and your enthusiasm will come back as you go through your cycle of success.

Thomas Edison's quote in reference to the process he went through to invent the light bulb sums this up perfectly: 'I have not failed. I've just found 10,000 ways that won't work.'

Find *your* 'balance' and live in the 'now'

Balance – not much in life is balanced. As women and mothers, we sometimes feel like we spend our lives running after everyone else and by the time we get to stop for the day, we're too exhausted to do anything for ourselves. Work/life balance is a foreign concept to me, but I have managed to introduce 'balance' into my life by prioritising, accepting that not everything on my 'to do' list will get done today, saying 'no' when I need to, and compartmentalising my time, among other strategies discussed in Chapter 4. I now feel like I have much more 'control' and this allows me to live in the present moment.

Living in the present moment is so beneficial to those around us and ourselves. If we are focused on what we are doing right now, such as reading this book instead of thinking about tonight's dinner (and then having to start reading the chapter again), we get more done and we feel better. The benefits include increased calm and decreased stress, improved immunity, and better control over the way we react to situations in life.

Stop multi-tasking and give what you are doing your undivided attention. If you don't live in the moment, when <u>will</u> you live?

Be kind to others and yourself

Give a little and you gain a lot. As you go about your day, consider how you can make someone else's day a little more pleasant? You may not have time to give, but you could contribute some money. You may not have money to give but you could contribute some time. Or you may simply thank or compliment someone. There are many ways to give to others. Please make service to others part of your life.

And while you're being kind to others don't forget about yourself. How critical we can be of ourselves – right? I think women are their own worst critics. ENOUGH! Let's start being nice to ourselves. Let's recognise that we do the best we can, we try and improve and each improvement is to be celebrated.

Sometimes, things are out of our control and yet we continue to strive and make things right with us, our family and friends and the world around us – if you think about it, that makes us pretty special human beings. Let's recognise that and love ourselves for it. Embrace the power of self-acceptance. We need to learn to love ourselves so we may truly know how to love others. BE KIND TO YOURSELF ALWAYS!

Focus on the great things about you and the things you can do. Keep adding to your 'I am awesome' list in your Wealth Creation Journal. We must take responsibility for the way we

Chapter 9: Bring It All Together And Make It Happen

feel about ourselves; we cannot rely on others to make us happy or to feel good about ourselves.

Be grateful for what you already have in your life, rather than focusing on what's missing. Take a few minutes each day to write down what you're grateful for. Enjoy each day even if you didn't appear to get closer to your goals. Always remember to cherish your moments with family and friends. Because these are the moments you remember most and the moments that others will remember when they think of you. You are exactly where you need to be right now. Be grateful for your past and be excited about your potential.

Never take anything for granted. Always be thankful! Always be grateful!

Opportunities are everywhere

When you put yourself on a path to achieve something, the universe appears to open up for you. Suddenly you will see opportunities that you didn't see before. For example, if you decided that you want to buy a red dress, you will suddenly start seeing red dresses everywhere. Of course you will be going into more dress shops as you look for your red dress, but this is all part of your mind helping you reach your goal. As you start talking to people about what you want to achieve, they will give you more ideas or assist in connecting you with people who can help. Achieving what you want is a team effort. You must let others know what you are striving for as people love to help when they can. The more you commit to your goals by telling people about them, the more you hold yourself accountable and make things happen.

As you focus on your goals you will find that opportunities are everywhere. New ideas will keep coming to you. Be open to your new ideas and let them build and grow. Every advancement we know of started as a small idea, followed by action until it finally became real. Don't underestimate your power when you develop new ideas. Thoughts become things.

Breaking through and achieving something significant is your pay off for your consistent hard work. Success in anything takes practice. Think of yourself like an athlete who is practicing the game of 'wealth creation' every day, and everyday you are becoming better and better at it and stronger and stronger at achieving your goals. Be patient with your learning curve and progress towards your goals.

> 'If you think in negative terms, you will get negative results. If you think in positive terms, you will get positive results.'
>
> ~ Norman Vincent Peale ~

Who's on your team?

As you begin your wealth creation journey, you will need the support of positive people who encourage and inspire you. Choose wisely who you spend time with and who you share your dreams with. Ask your family to be your cheerleaders and you theirs; praise and compliment their achievements, and thank them for supporting you. Focus on creating great

Chapter 9: Bring It All Together And Make It Happen

relationships with the significant people in your life – don't take anyone for granted. Oh, and don't get caught up in gossip and drama – there are enough people out there doing that.

As you start to formulate your income generating tasks and start to see some progress, you will need to develop a team of experts around you. You need to build your success team. This will initially be made up of people willing to help you for little or no money - friends and mentors to start with. You will eventually also need paid professionals on your team from accountants and bankers to advertising and web designers. Be on the look out for these people from the beginning, people you trust and admire who have complementary skills to you.

Integrity

As you take on new ventures and start creating the life of your dreams, have a pact with yourself to always do everything with integrity. If you are faced with dilemmas or difficult choices always ask yourself if they involve issues with integrity. If so, make a choice that you will always be able to look back on and be proud of. Plan in advance to have no regrets. That way even if things do not work out perfectly, at least you know you always did the right thing.

> 'Always do your best. What you plant now, you will harvest later.'
>
> ~ Og Mandino ~

From adversity comes valuable lessons

As you change and grow, there will be experiences that challenge you and push you out of your comfort zone. You will experience disappointment and sometimes feel defeated. Don't give up my friend. Look at these times as learning opportunities and remember that every 'NO' moves you closer to a 'YES'. Remember your 'Positive Mental Attitude' (See Chapter 1)? Choose how you will react to a situation, and turn 'lemons into lemonade'.

Always remember that it is life's journey and NOT the destination that is important.

> 'Every loss leads you to a gain, and every no takes you that much closer to a yes.'
>
> ~ Suze Orman ~

Leave a legacy

Every day – often without even realising - we are creating the legacy that we will leave to our friends, family and the wider community. A legacy comes in many forms from money or a bequest in a will; to the way we help people and touch their lives.

An author's legacy is his or her book and the impact it can have on someone's life. A sportsperson's legacy might be the inspiration they gave to young people to pursue their dream

Chapter 9: Bring It All Together And Make It Happen

of becoming a professional sportsperson or to stay fit and healthy. A singer's legacy is their songs and the way they make people feel. Your grandmother's legacy may be the memories you hold of her teaching you to cook or the words of wisdom she offered on your wedding day. A volunteer's legacy is the hours they donated to help a cause and the impact that had on something (e.g. the environment) or someone's life.

Oprah Winfrey has touched people's lives in many ways from the millions of dollars in donations through her Angel Network; to the education she is giving girls in South Africa at the Oprah Winfrey Leadership Academy for Girls. Her television shows have impacted the lives of millions of viewers who respected her honesty, authenticity and the information and education she brought into their homes.

If you've ever heard him speak or read one of his books you'll understand the inspiring legacy that Nick Vujicic is living. Born with no arms or legs, Nick travels the world speaking to audiences about how to overcome life's obstacles so they can achieve their dreams. Despite his physical handicaps he is cheerful, optimistic and inspiring.

Jane McGrath became a household name in Australia for her incredible efforts to raise awareness of breast cancer after she was diagnosed with the disease in 2002. Jane and cricketer husband Glenn McGrath established The McGrath Foundation, which raises money to fund McGrath Breast Cancer Nurses throughout Australia. Jane died in 2008 but her work continues to benefit women across the country every day.

I am committed to leaving a legacy that touches the lives of many. My hope is to donate more than $1 million to charity when I die, to have written a number of books that will inspire and teach people how to achieve their BEST life, and to inspire people through motivational talks and business coaching. My legacy will help to feed and clothe the poor in many countries around the world, and help to foster a community spirit and family togetherness.

What is your legacy?

> 'I don't think you ever stop giving. I really don't. I think it's an ongoing process. And it's not just about being able to write a cheque. It's being able to touch someone's life.'
>
> ~ Oprah Winfrey ~

My 10 final tips for YOU – mother, mum-to-be, single lady, married lady, businesswoman, career woman.

Before I sign off I want to leave you with 10 final tips to make your busy life that little bit more fun and manageable.

1. There is more to do than you can ever get done so only do those things you are passionate about or that really need doing.

Chapter 9: Bring It All Together And Make It Happen

2. Outsource. What tasks can you get others to do or share? For example, carpooling the kids for the school run or hiring a bookkeeper to do your taxes.

3. Planning. Sit down with the family and plan ahead. Schedule in the holidays and other priorities.

4. Cook healthy meals in advance – the slow cooker is perfect!

5. Schedule in exercise for your own health and wellbeing.

6. Make time for yourself and be sure to have a good night's sleep.

7. Dedicate time for fun with your family and friends – live in the moment and enjoy.

8. Practice the 90/10 rule. If you live well 90 per cent of the time it's okay to indulge on occasions.

9. Don't try to do everything at once. Multitasking is a great skill but it can make your head spin! Work in focused, short bursts.

10. Decide what you want your future to look like and start making it happen.

I want you to live an EXTRAORDINARY LIFE. Go make it happen!!!!

> 'May you live every day of your life.'
>
> ~ Jonathan Swift ~

Recommended reading

The One Minute Millionaire, Mark Victor Hansen

Having it all, John Assaraf

The Power of the Subconscious Mind, Dr Joseph Murphy

You were Born Rich, Bob Proctor

The Answer, John Assaraf and Murray Smith

Life Without Limits: Inspiration for a Ridiculously Good Life, Nick Vujicic

O's Big Book of Happiness – The Best of O, Oprah Magazine Editors

Stay in touch

I'd love to stay in touch and hear your incredible stories of change and success! Please contact me through my website www.extraordinaryyou.net so we can see the change you are making in the world.

I also welcome your comments and accomplishments on our Facebook page http://www.facebook.com/megan.wolfendens.page

Appendix 1: Book Club

At the end of each chapter you will find a list of books that have been inspirational to me and helped keep me on my track to living an extraordinary life. When I was 19 my brother gave me a copy of *Your Erroneous Zones* by Wayne W Dyer. I have to admit that I started reading it because I misunderstood and thought it was 'Your Erogenous Zones'. It didn't take long for me to recognise my error but I kept reading and found the book sensational. That was my first personal development book. From then on I read lots and lots of personal development books.

Then in my 30s my mother-in-law gave me *Rich Dad Poor Dad* by Robert Kiyosaki. That began my true financial education. Since that time I have followed a simple routine of reading two to three educational books followed by a non-fiction, FUN book as a treat to myself. If you use the local library, reading is FREE and the education you get out of reading is priceless. One of my good friends says, 'The more you learn, the more you earn'. In fact after a seminar with Robert Kiyosaki I wrote a short recommendation about the course and it was published in his brochure. A long lost friend working at the same company as me, saw that brochure and read my testimonial and contacted me. She said, 'I want to take you out to lunch and hear what you have to say about these courses because I might go to one'. We began meeting regularly to share what we were learning about business and investing. She then got permission from our company and set up a once a month lunchtime meeting for people wanting to know more about investing. She brought in professionals to talk to us free of charge about their areas of expertise and before long we had 40 people in the group. She and I were able to retire from that company because of our network marketing incomes but the group is still in existence and going strong.

For these reasons I recommend you share this book with a couple of girlfriends and then set up your own book club focused on personal development, business and investing. To start with you may want to read the books recommended in each chapter of this book. More recommendations can be found at www.extraordinaryyou.net.

I recommend a club of six to eight people that meet once a month, rotating the meeting place among the member's homes. Everyone should read the same book each month and when you get together you talk about what you learnt from the book. Take notes and after a couple of months you will find that you want to take action on what you are learning. Members of the group may go to different seminars and come back to the group and give a summary of what they have learnt. If the lead up to the holidays is very busy and the group doesn't think anyone can finish a book that month then as a group buy Robert Kiyosaki's Rich Dad Cashflow 101 game and play that instead. This game should be played over and over. It would be fun to have a get together with partners to Play Cashflow 101 as well. This game really brings couples together on their financial education and helps them work as a team to 'Get out of the rat race'. I spent this past week at the snow with my family and one of my successful girlfriends. I asked her when it was that she decided to 'take action' and start creating her successful investment portfolio. She said that her and her husband were invited to a friend's house to play Cashflow 101 and they continued playing once a month for many months. After the sixth time playing the game they finally realised that they were not getting ahead financially doing what they were doing so they had to make changes. Their first investment was a block of four apartments near their hometown in California. This was a very successful purchase and was the beginning of their successful real estate portfolio. They have also gone on to become successful network marketers and investors.

Write and tell us your group or individual success stories. We LOVE to hear of people's success and how you put it all together. We want YOU to inspire others to lead extraordinary lives.

Write to successsstories@extraordinaryyou.net and tell us what you are doing to live the life of your dreams. We want to hear your trials, mistakes and wins so others can learn from you.

> 'Education is not preparation for life; education is life itself.'
>
> ~ John Dewey ~

Appendix 2: Recommended Reading List

Book/ Audio Title	Author	Ordered On	Completed on
Having it All	John Assaraf		
The Answer	John Assaraf and Murray Smith		
Like a Virgin – Secrets they wont teach you at Business School	Sir Richard Branson		
Sorting out Self-Esteem	Grant Brecht		
The Go-Giver	Bob Burg and John David Mann		
Australia's Money Secrets of the Rich	John Burley		
The Secret	Rhonda Byrne		
Jack Canfield's Key to Living the Law of Attraction: A Simple Guide to Creating the Life of Your Dreams	Jack Canfield		
Chicken Soup for the Soul	Jack Canfield and Mark Victor Hansen		

Appendix 2: Recommended Reading List

Book/ Audio Title	Author	Ordered On	Completed on
Don't sweat the small stuff…and it's all small stuff	Richard Carlson		
How to Win Friends and Influence People	Dale Carnegie		
Creating Affluence – the A to Z steps to a richer life	Deepak Chopra		
The Seven Spiritual Laws of Success: A Practical Guide to the Fulfilment of Your Dreams	Deepak Chopra		
Richest Man in Babylon	George S. Clason		
Giving	Bill Clinton		
What you think of me is none of my business?	Terry Cole-Whittaker		
The 7 Habits of Happy Kids	Sean Covey and Stacy Curtis		
Simple Changes – Your 100 ways to a happier, Healthier Life	Philip Day		

Book/ Audio Title	Author	Ordered On	Completed on
Count your Blessings: The Healing Power of Gratitude and Love	Dr John F Demartini		
Real Magic: Creating Miracles in Everyday Life	Wayne W. Dyer		
The 4-Hour Workweek	Timothy Ferriss		
The Busy Family's Guide to Volunteering: Doing Good Together	Jenny Friedman		
Creative Visualization	Shakti Gawain		
Outliers	Malcolm Gladwell		
The Power of Awareness	Neville Goddard		
Men Are from Mars, Women Are from Venus: The Classic Guide to Understanding the Opposite Sex	John Gray		

Appendix 2: Recommended Reading List

Book/ Audio Title	Author	Ordered On	Completed on
Children are from Heaven	John Gray		
The One Minute Millionaire	Mark Victor Hansen		
You Can Heal Your Life	Louise L Hay		
How to love yourself	Louise L. Hay		
Think and Grow Rich	Napoleon Hill		
Instant Wealth Wake Up Rich! Discover The Secret of The New Entrepreneurial Mind	Christopher Howard		
Feel the Fear and Do it Anyway	Susan Jeffers		
Health & Wellbeing Millionaire	Fiona Jones & Rebecca Griffin with Paul Scicluna		
Property Millionaire	Fiona Jones and Nhan Nguyen		
The Business of the 21st Century	Robert Kiyosaki		

Book/ Audio Title	Author	Ordered On	Completed on
Rich Dad Poor Dad	Robert Kiyosaki		
Rich Woman	Kim Kiyosaki		
Put More Cash in Your Pocket: Turn What You Know into Dough	Loral Langemeier		
The Millionaire Maker: Act, Think and Make Money the Way the Wealthy Do	Loral Langemeier		
Personality Plus: How to Understand Others by Understanding Yourself	Florence Littauer		
You Inc	John McGrath		
The Power of the Subconsious Mind	Dr Joseph Murphy		
O's Big Book of Happiness – The Best of O	Oprah Magazine Editors		

Appendix 2: Recommended Reading List

Book/ Audio Title	Author	Ordered On	Completed on
Dr. Perricone's 7 Secrets to Beauty, Health, and Longevity: The Miracle of Cellular Rejuvenation	M.D. Nicholas Perricone		
You were Born Rich	Bob Proctor		
Awaken the Giant Within	Anthony Robbins		
Lean In	Sheryl Sandberg		
Happy for no Reason	Marci Shimoff		
Ageless: The Naked Truth About Bioidentical Hormones	Suzanne Somers		
The Millionaire Next Door	Thomas Stanley and William Danko		
The Secret of Vigor	Dr Shawn Talbott		
Your Mark on the World	Devin Thorpe		
The Farmacists Desk Reference	Don Tolman		

Book/ Audio Title	Author	Ordered On	Completed on
Why We Want to be Rich	Donald Trump and Robert Kiyosaki		
Life Without Limits: Inspiration for a Ridiculously Good Life	Nick Vujicic		
Five Stages of Health	Dr Ross Walker		
Superfoods: The food and medicine of the future	David Wolfe		
Your First Year in Network Marketing	Mark Yanell		
Selling 101	Zig Ziglar		

www.ingramcontent.com/pod-product-compliance
Lightning Source LLC
Chambersburg PA
CBHW050632300426
44112CB00012B/1759